THE **GREAT DRAMA**
OF **HUMAN LIFE**

THE **GREAT DRAMA**
OF **HUMAN LIFE**

REVEREND HUGH COWAN

THE GREAT DRAMA OF HUMAN LIFE

Published By: Silverwoods Publishing - a division of McK Consulting Inc.
Toronto ~ Windsor ~ Chicago

ISBN: 978-1-897202-19-7

CONTENTS

An Historical Survey of the Progress of the World Christward during the last half-century, with a forecast of what Christendom will be believing and teaching at the close of the present half-century, concerning
THE DESTINY OF THE HUMAN FAMILY.

In the beginning years of his Christian ministry.

THE AUTHOR

A student for thirty-six years of Christian thought, who believes that in the Christ-concept of the Soul of God and the God-created Potentiality of Man, we have the clue to the Truth concerning the Destiny of the Human Family:

Who believes, also, that the Achievement of the world-wide Brotherhood, prophesied by Christ, is the premier Duty of present-day Christendom.

INTRODUCTION

THIS WORK WAS written and published by my great-grand-father, Reverend Hugh Cowan in 1937. I never met him as he died fifteen years before I was born. My great-grand-mother Jean Eloise Wood Cowan was a positive and pleasant person through my childhood years. I enjoyed reading his books, articles, and some letters that still exist. As well, I have visited most of the churches that he served during his years of ministry. I share many of his interests including ministry, history and the world of words, though I am a lesser heir of a greater sire in his case and that of my many colourful ances-tors. His love of the areas of Muskoka and Georgian Bay also was passed down to me as well.

As a discussion of the theology of his time, this book resonates with many of the great questions that are still part of theological discourse today. I also found some of the anecdotes and stories that illustrated his life as a minister to be as fascinating as the theological topics. His observations and reflections on his faith journey tell me more about who he was as much as what he believed.

By the time he published this book, he was retired. As with the earlier Ontario histories, it appears that he planned to do a series of books. Perhaps with advancing age and then the beginning of WWII, that became more ambition than real possibility.

As copies of this book are few and far between, it seemed like a book to have reprinted for family and those interested in the topic. The content of the book is as it was originally self-published under his own copyright.

It is a snapshot of debate of his time, informed by his study and life of ministry. The fact that it addresses issues that are still relevant today speaks to both his thought and to the great drama of human life that continues for our generation just as it did for his.

Thanks to each of the family members who have encouraged our connection with those Cowans and others who went before us. Special appreciation goes to Jennifer Alvarez for the transcription of the book. The book formatting was the work of Jeny Lyn Ruelo. The cover design was by my wife, Cari Fairley. Featured on the cover is the stained glass window of Rutherford Presbyterian Church near Dresden, Ontario. The first churches that Hugh Cowan served as a minister was a twin charge of Rutherford and Oakdale Presbyterian Churches. It was at Rutherford that Hugh Cowan met and married his wife, Jean Eloise Wood, from nearby Langbank, Ontario. Nine children and the service many different churches over the years would follow before the writing of this book.

Grant D. Fairley
January 2014

FOREWORD

THIS WORLD'S A stage, a poet once sung, and on it each man must act his part. Another poet has said, "Change and decay in all around I see."

Two poets, one sees in human life a great drama, and every member of the human family performing a part in that drama; the other sees in human life, change and death.

In the great drama of human life, the producer of the drama is God; the Lord Jesus supplies to the stage its light; while the Spirit of God is the One who trains and disciplines and practises the actors so that each may do their part wisely and well, even perfectly. The members of the human family, the actors on the stage, some do their part wisely and well, never perfectly; some do their part not so wisely and not so well; others do not do their part at all; while still others are out in rebellion to destroy the good influence and effect of the drama, if they can.

In accord with this viewpoint of the human family, there has come down to us through the ages the teaching, that the destiny of the first two classes of these actors at death is Paradise, while the other two classes of the human family are doomed to a place of torment, or torture, named by the Greeks, *Gehenna*, and by the Jews, *Hades*.

About fifty years ago, there began a movement which has all the years since steadily advanced, has caught the ear of public opinion, and is so to-day determining the beliefs of an increasing number of followers, a movement which challenges this teaching, and, instead, stresses the Christ-concept of God as "Our Father," and all the deductions which legitimately follow from that concept.

This movement, as it came under our own personal observation, is the subject of this treatise, which we are submitting to the public with the hope that it will aid, even in a small measure, to draw their attention to what has been taking place in the realm of Christian thought during this fifty-year period.

PRAYER

OUR FATHER, WHO dwellest in, but who art greater than, the great universe which Thou hast created, our spirit contemplates with sacred reverence the greatness of Thy power, a power which Thou art exercising to-day, to make of each unit of the human race, Thy marvelous creation, a temple of Love.

We surrender our souls now unto Thee, praying that in the deeper depths of our nature Thou wilt exercise that great power, that we may be moulded in our spirit like unto Thyself, for Thou art the God of Love, its Creator, and the only source from which we can imbibe and become partners with Thee in its possession.

Honour Thyself, we humbly and reverently, but hopefully, pray, by granting to us a baptism of that Gracious Spirit, that we may walk under the guidance of its influence all our lives.—Amen.

THE TEMPLE OF CHRISTIAN TRUTH

ALL THE WORLD once believed that the earth was flat. They believe so no longer. The idea that it was spherical in shape was released by some thinker of the human family, who either reasoned it out for himself, or it was given to him as an intuition of his mind. Other men listened, heard the reasons for his belief, and being convinced of their cogency, joined with him in his belief. The number of his followers so increased that, at last, not one intelligent member throughout the whole human family could be found who believed anything other than that the earth was a sphere. It was the truth, discovered by this one man, which drove out the error so long cherished before by a unanimous world.

Almost two thousand years ago, Christ came to this world to tell us what was true, concerning the destiny of man. On the last day of His earthly life, He made declaration to a Roman pagan of the nature and motive of His mission:

"For this cause came I unto the world, that I should bear witness to the truth."

"What is truth?" queried this Roman pagan, voicing in this the all-important question, the answer to which means so much to human prosperity, human progress, human happiness and human life.

To this question, Jesus made no answer. An open mind and a heart sympathetic with the truth is an essential condition to know the truth. This pagan's mind was closed to the truth. His heart was not sympathetic with it. Hence, in view of this, Jesus maintained a discreet silence.

So also was it in respect to his own countrymen. The Jewish nation, as a nation, refused to accept his teaching. They had a religious system which might be termed the constitution of their nation. Their national life became the expression of it. They revered it with a tenacity of pride and a conservatism of thought which forbade any reflection on its perfection and completeness. Any of their countrymen who would suggest change or improvement, they would deem guilty of sedition, a traitor to his country.

Jesus was raised up and divinely commissioned, not to destroy the system, but to bring to it added enlightenment, such enlightenment as would change it from a national to a world-wide religious system. In His teaching He laid emphasis on certain concepts concerning God and His laws, not new and unheard—of concepts, but those which had been before taught and more or less appreciated during the whole period of Jewish history. Upon this fuller interpretation and wider application of them the Jewish nation looked first with suspicious dissent, gradually increasing in its animosity until it became, finally, virulent hate. They killed the teacher, but His teaching remained, since, being the truth it was impossible to destroy it.

That teaching has not as yet received from the generations of mankind the consideration and honest interpretation which its merit deserves. The question asked by the Children of Israel on the first morning when the bread of heaven lay in plenteous supply on the ground about their tents—WHAT IS IT?—that question has been asked by succeeding generations since concerning the teaching of Christ, but notwithstanding that two millenniums of years have elapsed since the Word dwelt among us, the knowledge of that teaching possessed by the world has been very imperfect; their interpretation of it in many instances false; their loyalty to it insincere; and their application of it in some instances brutally cruel.

If we look for unanimity as to what comprises Christian truth, we shall be much disappointed. Should one generation become practically unanimous in respect to the interpretation of one of His major topics, it would be only to produce a stagnation in thought with a subsequent generation discovering incompleteness and imperfections in their pronouncements. Nevertheless, the sum-total of two thousand years' trial of the Christian system, and the teachings of Jesus in respect to it, has resulted, it is generally believed, in a steady advance and progress both Godward and truthward. The present century finds us passing through one of those stages of trial and progress. This movement has new crystallized itself into a definite clear-cut faith, a summarized statement of which we herewith subjoin under the title "The New-thought schoolmen: their seven axioms of Christian truth."

These seven axioms, we take it, fairly represent the thinking of present-day Christendom. They outline a faith advanced in several particulars over the faith of fifty years ago. Commencing with the first, which expresses the Christ-concept of the Soul of God, the most vital of all the topics with which religion has to do, they follow one another in successive order.

AXIOMS OF CHRISTIAN TRUTH

FIRST: THAT GOD, the Father of all mankind, is loving, forgiving, merciful; a Father to be loved, not a judge to be feared.

Second: That Christ Jesus is the Enlightener of the world; that to Him we must look for the truth concerning the Soul of God, the Potentiality of Man, and the Destiny of Man; the truth of all those ideas, thoughts and concepts, which belong to the realm of faith; that in His Resurrection, together with the subsequent experiences of His followers, we have the confirmation of the truth of His teachings; that these, therefore, are a safe guide in all matters relating to the realm of faith; that the Cross was not an atonement for sin, but the price which He had to pay for loyalty to truth, and therefore the emblem of His life sacrificed in behalf of the truth.

Third: That the Spirit of God, in relation to the salvation of man, is not a power outside of man, making periodical visits to this earth; not a power which comes to man only at his conversion; but that it is an ENERGY which comes into the life of every new-born babe on the day of its birth, abiding with that babe, the ENERGIZER Within its little life, enabling it to grow in the likeness of God in which it was created in potentiality; that this Spirit of indwelling in every member of the human family, and associated as the Energizer in every relationship of the family life, you can grieve, you can disobey, but you cannot quench, neither in this life nor in the life to come.

Fourth: That man is dual in his nature; that he possesses both a nature-life and a spirit-life: that in his spirit-life he is created in the image of God, but in his nature-life, in its origin, preservation, and continuance he is made subject to the laws of the material universe.

That man is born a potentiality to become perfect, even as perfect as God would have him be, and that each member of the human family will realize his potentiality, not one excepted.

Sixth: That the human family is a unity; that there is a oneness, a solidarity which makes a happening to one be a happening to all, and the responsibility of one be the responsibility of all; that all the relationships of the members one towards another are based on potentiality in love; and that the Spirit of God, as in each individual member, so also in the family, is the Energizer, inspiring men to respect, to regard, to love one another; inspiring men to "have a heart," when others of their fellowmen are in trouble or in need.

Seventh: "That when a man dies, the disintegration of his nature-life does not affect his spirit-life; that after death there is an unbroken continuance of his spirit-life under conditions suited to the carrying out of the realization of his potentiality; that he will continue to move forward from stage to stage in progress until he has achieved the goal set for man, — "Be ye perfect, even as your heavenly Father is perfect"; and that this will be true of every member of the human family, not one excepted."

Upward, onward upward,
Moves the human race,
As their star recedeth
To its heav'nly place.

'Tis the urge of nature;
'Tis the will divine;
Upward, onward upward,
So our hearts incline.

Upward, onward upward,
To yon heav'nly throne,
Higher and still higher
Till the crown's your own.

There's no mower valley,
There's no humbler place;
To that height celestial
Follow with your race.

THOUGHT-IDEAS, FAITH-CONCEPTS, FOOL-THOUGHTS

THE HUMAN MIND creates certain thoughts, ideas and concepts concerning human life and its destiny. Interchange of these is made possible through a language which is also the creation of human intelligence. Terms are used to express these ideas, thoughts and concepts, which unfortunately do not always convey the same meaning to all persons alike. Our language, is therefore, whether written or spoken, at very imperfect medium to convey our thoughts and ideas to others. Especially is this true in respect to ideas and concepts on the subject of religion and Christianity.

In this treatise, we make frequent use of terms concerning the nature of man and God, which we should perhaps, at the start, define, in order to lessen the likelihood of the reader having a different thought concerning the meaning of these terms than that which the author would seek to convey. This is all the more necessary since we are using some words in a narrower or different sense from their commonly accepted use. Of such is the word Christendom, which we use to signify the English-speaking branches of the Christian church. In this way we may arrive at a clarified idea as to what we mean by the Temple of Christian Truth, and the best methods which we should follow in the creation of such a temple.

We have, therefore, divided the concepts, ideas and thoughts entering into our temple of Christian truth into three classes, according to the source from which we derived them, naming them respectively:

1. Thought-Ideas.
2. Faith-Concepts
3. Fool-Thoughts.

We come to a knowledge of the first, a thought-idea, through our own unaided intelligence. Having carefully considered it and weighed all the data available confirming it, if we are then satisfied as to its verity, we accept it as true, and in all our thinking afterwards it becomes a part of our storehouse of Truth. The idea that the earth turns round on its axis once in every twenty—four hours is a thought-idea, obtained by sense and reason, and once discovered remains ever after a part of our mental equipment.

The second, the faith-concept, belongs to a class which comprises the major part of all our concepts. This is a concept which is discovered by an intelligence other than our own. This may be the intelligence of one of our fellowmen, who, by reason of possessing a higher-developed or a better-furnished mind than ours, or because he has been placed in circumstances more favoured, is able to discover truth in fields of knowledge not immediately available to us.

A faith-idea is an advance over a thought-idea in that it possesses an additional quality interwoven with it and a part of it. This additional element is a trust, a confidence in the person who has brought this concept within range of our knowledge and made it possible for us to incorporate it into and make it a part of our temple of knowledge. It carries also with it the assurance that he, out of his superior intelligence, knows it to be true. He being altogether trustworthy in respect to his ability to observe, to conceive and to corroborate what he has observed and conceived, we arrive at a truth which we could not possibly have discovered apart from this service rendered to us by the one in whom we have thus placed our confidence. The knowledge on which a child directs its life is faith-knowledge. So also is the knowledge which we possess concerning the food value of certain products of the soil. We act on the testimony of others.

We do this because of our faith. If we lacked this faith we would pass over their thought-idea, giving no heed to it. Having that faith, it is as if we had seen and thought out the idea for ourselves. We accept what their eyes have seen, what their ears have heard, what their minds have thought, as though we had seen and heard and thought it out for ourselves. This could be only because we believed and trusted and had confidence in them; and that they, on their part, were worthy of that trust.

The ideas, thoughts and concepts released and taught by Christ concerning God and the kingdom of God belong to this class. These, to have any value for us, will have to carry with them a trust in Him as a teacher "sent from God." We shall have to have a confidence in the truth of them and the assurance that their truth will be confirmed by the experiences which shall later come to pass in our life.

All the ideas, concepts and thoughts which we have gathered and stored away in our Temple of Truth are not always true, though we may think that they are. The earth was flat for all the people of the earth for many generations. Hence we have another class of concepts, a class which belongs to an entirely different realm from either of the two already mentioned, a class to which we have given the name of fool-thoughts, The term has been suggested to us by a statement from the Holy Scriptures, "The fool hath said in his heart, There is no God." As a man thinketh in his heart, so is he. Here we find a man cherishing a false idea concerning the most important reality of life. If we are wrong here we are wrong in everything in life. If our mental vision is out of focus here, everything we see we shall see distorted, crooked, untrue.

The fool-thought maintains that to be true which is not true and that which is untrue to be true. Why should anyone make affirmation that there is no God? Is it that the data have not been supplied by which the truth of God's existence could be made known to us and proved to be true? Or, possessing the data, has man been denied the intelligence which will enable him to appreciate and make proper use of the available data? Though man so bereft could not be accounted responsible, nevertheless the concept itself would remain false and the product of a fool's brain.

There being a possibility of retaining fool-thoughts in our storehouse of knowledge, every concept, even our faith-concepts, should be passed through the crucible of our own intelligence to be tested and confirmed, no matter how reliable may be the source from which we originally derived them. It is not What we believe true which makes us disciples of truth, but What we have confirmed true by the experiences through which we were subsequently called upon to pass. If a concept bears the car-marks of being a fool-thought, a wise man will immediately set out to obtain evidence, if this is available, to determine its class. If discovered false, he will at once discard it. If not discarded, his integrity and potency are immediately and in that measure discounted.

The mind of man is so created by God that it demands of itself the data, the confirmation. It will not take the mere word of another unless there is no data available with which he can corroborate it for himself.

A teacher of science places two jars on a table before a class of his students and informs them that one of the jars contains oxygen gas, but the other nitrogen gas. The students see nothing. Naturally their minds are not satisfied. They desire confirmatory evidence. To meet their wish, the teacher takes a splinter of cedar on the end of which there is a small spark of fire. He plunges it into the jar said to contain oxygen gas. Immediately it is all in a blaze. He plunges the blazing splinter into the other jar. Immediately it goes out. The minds of the students are now satisfied. He has convinced them that his statement was true and that in the one jar there was that which supported combustion because it was oxygen, but that in the other jar there was that which had the opposite property, being nitrogen.

It is not truth alone, as we said, which makes our belief to be true faith, but truth confirmed. Unconfirmed belief is mere credulity and nothing more. Hence we must use all available material to confirm the truth behind our beliefs lest, cherishing what we suppose to be a faith-concept, we are instead cherishing a fool-thought. Neglecting an essential duty, we may come to a wrong conclusion respecting its nature and quality, a position dishonouring to truth, to God and to ourselves.

A boy came home from high-school one evening tired and with some fever. He did this for several evenings, when he was urged by his mother to consult a physician. The physician knew it to be one of two diseases, fever or tuberculosis. He did not make use of all the data available, but jumped to the conclusion that it was fever. After he had waited the allotted thirty days, he discovered that it was not what he thought it to be, but the other. The boy died. Would he have died if the physician had made a right diagnosis in the first instance? The sanitarium unto which the boy was sent believed that he would not.

Influenza became an epidemic in a certain neighbourhood. Children with weeping eyes and sore throats were everywhere in evidence. A physician was called to visit one of the homes, the father being absent, and discovered all these symptoms. He pronounced it influenza. On the father's return to his home he at once recognized it to be scarlet fever. The physician, recalled, confirmed the father's judgment. Immediately the physician rushed to another home where he had made a similar diagnosis for similar symptoms. Two boys were being treated. One died. Would he have died if the mistake in diagnosis had not been made? The physician himself believed he would not. Confirmation there must be when confirmation is possible. It is only thus we shall save ourselves from being the victims of a fool-thought concerning the destiny of man; and, cherishing a wrong viewpoint of the goal of human life, suffer its blasting influence upon our character and life.

THE DESTINED GOAL OF THE HUMAN RACE

WHAT CAN WE KNOW concerning human life? And, what can we know concerning human destiny?

We can know some things concerning human life from observation. Concerning the destiny of man we can know only what we are told. Concerning human life, we can have thought ideas, discovered or created through the exercise of our own intelligence, for human life comes under the observation of our senses. Concerning the destiny of man, we can have only faith—concepts. These we must have revealed to us by God, or through the agencies which He has set up to reveal the truth concerning our destiny to us. In the one we are in the realm of knowledge; in the other we are in the realm of faith. Of the one, we can say "I know"; of the other we cannot say this, only, "I believe."

Due, in the first place, to the discoveries of Science in the realm of nature:

Due, in the second place, to the emphasis which has been laid by Christian thought on the Soul of as revealed by Christ:

Due, in a marked degree, in the third place, to a new concept of the nature and potentiality of man:

Due to these three, and doubtless other reasons, there began, about fifty years ago, a marked trend away from formerly accepted teachings of Christendom concerning the destiny of man, a definite swing of Christian thought away from the immediately former standards of faith concerning the life of man beyond the grave; one of those critical movements which has caught the ear of public opinion, has all the years since steadily advanced, and is now determining the belief of an increasing number of followers.

Up until about half a century ago, there was an almost undivided opinion concerning the destiny of man, an almost unbroken sameness of faith. If, meeting ten men on the street at that period of time, you made inquiry whether or not they believed in the punishment of the wicked after death in a place called Gehenna, or Hades, you would receive invariably an answer in the affirmative. Follow the same procedure to-day, and the answer would be an emphatic negative from nine of them at least. Is this change of viewpoint to be labeled retrogression, or progress? Shall we call it a departure from the faith? Or shall we name it a more enlightened faith? Shall we point to it as an advance of Christian thought one stage further truthward? Or shall we declare it to be a baneful departure from well-founded Christian belief? Concerning this question, we have three schools of thought, each with its own answer and faith.

In the first of these three we find, not so much a faith, as the absence of faith. The representatives of this school declare that the end awaiting all men is annihilation, an event which will occur at death. The death of the nature-life means the death of the spirit-life. When the last breath is drawn, when the physician lifts up his hand and announces to those around, "He is dead," there has come to man a cessation of all being, both of the nature-life and the spirit-life, both in respect to this world and the world to come.

"There shall no soul on the ship be saved."

According to the professed belief of the Annihilationist school, this is the end of all men.

The second faith, the one which has held sway these many eras, carrying the thinking of the English-speaking Christendom with it, divides the human family into two classes, the "saved" and the "lost." A veritable paradise is awaiting one division of the family, according to this faith, but the experience which we call death, dooms the members of the other division to a place of torture, a place of punishment, called by the Greeks, Gehenna, but by the Jews, Hades. In this place of punishment they remain aeon after aeon, suffering the tortures which their ill lives upon this earth merited for them, and from which after death there is no escape. From this fate, the "saved," the first division, escape because of an unmerited grace of God; but, instead, there is bestowed upon them the gift of eternal bliss in an abode of happiness, a place specially prepared for them, where they dwell forever in the enjoyment of this unmerited grace of God.

The third faith, that of the school which throughout this treatise is called the New—thought school, the one whose short history of fifty years we are now chronicling, challenges the viewpoint of both of those above—mentioned schools, claiming that the end of our earthly life leads every member of the human family, not one excepted, into another life which will be a fuller, a more glorious, a more perfect life than the one which we lived here; where the realization of the potentiality of man, achieved in a measure in his earthly career, will be continued on under more favourable and happy conditions in the next stage of his being. Released from certain limitations, necessarily attached to our earthly existence, mankind will live in this new place of abode, the happy participants of a fuller measure of love than it was here possible for them to enjoy. There will be no cessation in their progressive march onward towards the achievement of the goal set by the Divine Mind for their attainment—"Be ye perfect, even as your heavenly Father is perfect"—until that goal is achieved and that for the whole of the human family, not one excepted.

While we have said that this third school has had attached to it as yet, only a fifty-year history, it would be difficult to say just when the movement first commenced. In our own

Canadian church, and our observations are confined to Christian progress in Canada, it probably received public attention first in connection with the ministry of the Rev. D. J. MacDonnell of New Saint Andrew's Presbyterian Church, Toronto. In the course of a sermon which he was preaching, he quoted a verse from a widely-read secular poet of his day, in which the thought was suggested that the Whole of mankind, not one excepted, was moving towards one ultimate goal of good. Apart from this quotation, and whatever remarks the preacher may have made relative to it, the sermon was otherwise quite orthodox.

The concept of the poet, in the judgment of some that listened, was deemed heresy, and Mr. MacDonnell was deemed his disciple by reason of his having made this quotation. He was hauled before his Presbytery to explain or defend himself. Submitting that he had made no statement, either for or against the idea contained in the poem, the Presbytery declared that a case had not been made out against him.

Following shortly after this, a certain Professor Campbell of Montreal was before his Presbytery also, and on a similar charge. He apparently went a step further than Mr. MacDonnell, for although he was not convicted of heresy, his remarks concerning the possibility of the doctrine of Hades being perhaps some day discarded, were considered indiscreet, and a resolution, embodying a mild censure, was endorsed by the Presbytery.

It was about this time also, that the Rev. Dr. Henry Drummond, that modern apostle of love, inspired perhaps by the discoveries which secular students were making in the field of physical science, came forward with a treatise in which he sought to show that those laws which scientists were discovering in physical nature, that these applied also in the realm of the spiritual. This being granted, especially in respect to the Law of Evolution, the possibility of Gehenna, or Hades, would be precluded.

Altogether, there began an observed movement in the top branches of the poplars, and men, both inside the church and out, were wont to query, "What meaneth this?"

But if these three Christian gentlemen prefixed their remarks with a "perhaps," not so their disciples.

"This meaneth," these said, "that we are now discovering the Christ-concept of God – that 'God is "Our Father," loving, forgiving, merciful, a Father to be loved, not a Judge to be feared,' and that therefore a destiny of torture for anyone of His children, is quite impossible and unthinkable. The units of the human family who have become victims of Evil, these are proper subjects for a heavenly clinic, not for an angry God's guillotine of torture."

Announcing themselves, not secret, but avowed disciples of the Christ-concept of God as "Our Father," and all the deductions which logically follow from this concept, they declare that the doctrine of Gehenna, or Hades, is not a proper article of the Christian faith, a concept, not only incompatible with the Christ-concept of God as "Our Father," but a concept as cruel and childish as was the pagan mind which first gave it birth.

It might not be inappropriate to observe here that Reverend D. J. MacDonnell, Professor Campbell and Doctor Drummond were all three of them reputed to be men of very tender, loving and sympathetic natures — natures which made it hard for them to believe in a tortured future as the destined end of any of their fellowmen. Natures callous and cruel find it easy to believe in Gehenna. Perhaps in this we may find a clue, both as to the origin of the doctrine in the first place and its continuance in popular favour by theologians and religious doctrinaires these many centuries since.

Having this in view, we doubt very much if this phase of New-thought teaching will receive that ready acceptance which some of their other teachings received. The belief in force and punishment as requisites, essential for maintaining order in human society, has become so entrenched in the human mind that it will be very difficult to have it uprooted. An order of society in which force and punishment are not found is beyond their comprehension, and, therefore, an object neither of their desires nor expectations. Nevertheless, a social order in which either force or punishment will not be found and where, moreover, they will not be needed, is the goal set for human achievement by the Divine Mind and Plan of the Ages.

This lack of expectation and desire finds strong support when fortified by a standard of character in which an element of cruelty is strongly entrenched. As I write, the morning newspaper on my desk contains an illuminating example of this entrenched cruelty. It tells how, a few weeks ago, a Hamilton city mother brought her son to the local public schoolmaster and said, "We can do nothing with him. Can you?"

The master took him in hand, determined he would instill "character" into his nature. It was not long until the boy put his will up against the teacher's, as he had previously done against his mother's. Punishment, in which pain and hurt, cruelty and torture, and destruction of living tissue, this because he wanted the liberty to exercise his own individuality and to carry out the thought and will of his own purpose, was administered to his body in a most shameless and brutal manner, and this in the year of grace, 1937.

The incident aroused public indignation, and the teacher was brought before the local magistrate. The teacher was acquitted of the charge cruelty and commended.

"We must have discipline," was the comment of the officer, justifying his decision.

Reason and the grace of love found no place in this method of achieving a well-regulated social order. Is this the Christ-concept of what should be the proper relationship of man to man, and of parent and master to child?

Consider our own Doukhobor problem. Here we have an immigration originally numbering seven thou sand forty years ago, but by this time greatly increased, professing Christians, believing in one God, and, though looking upon Christ as the Son of God in the same sense as all men are sons of God, yet claim that only by his indwelling in their hearts are they saved. Centuries of persecution have made them like their persecutors, hard, suspicious, intractable, intolerant, cruel, having no faith whatever in their fellowman outside of their own commune. It will take generations to make of them good

Canadian citizens. A programme of force and punishment will not, however, assimilate them. Kindness, consideration, patience, love—this, on the testimony of the teachers sent out among them, is the only method of lifting them to the present-day standard of Christian thought and life.

THE SOUL OF GOD

ALL THE BRANCHES of organized Christianity are one of their belief that Jesus, if he did not teach anything else, taught that God is "Our Father."

If they are in disagreement concerning other concepts of God taught by Christ, they are not in this. They have unanimously placed this teaching as an article in their creedal beliefs, not one of them excepted. They have incorporated it into their prayer books, not one excepted. When they open their Bibles, it is at the place where it is written, "When ye pray, say, 'Our Father.'"

The idea of God as "Our Father" revealed to us by the Master Mind of Nazareth, ascribes to Him three attributes each bearing an important relationship in respect to the destiny of man. This is the concept of Him as a good and kindly Father, perfect in His love, perfect in His forgiving grace, and perfect in His forgiving mercy.

These three attributes of His nature find each their outlet for expression in the needs of the human family. They need love; they need forgiveness; they need His pitying mercy. Therefore He bestows it upon all without exception, because they fill need it.

This concept represents Him to us as having a power to love even the most degraded, the most ugly-natured of the human family, even the criminals and the derelicts. He sees their departures from true life and manhood only with pitying mercy, and a purposed mind to restore and make them whole.

This being the soul of God, no longer do the sinful need to approach Him with fear in their hearts, for He is not, as the concept of the old-thought school pictured, waiting with anger in His spirit and a sword in His hand to mete out the punishment which their ill-lives merited. Nay, instead, they may approach Him as "Father," alert in the observance of the needs of His children, basting to their aid when required, and bearing towards them at all times à spirit of forgiveness and compassionate mercy.

This concept of Him stands in its very nature different from all other prevailing concepts. What the issue of human life is going to be would never be known to us, unless He revealed Himself to us as "Our Father," declared by Christ to be the true concept of Him, a revealing of Himself to us by deeds of love, of forgiveness and of mercy. Does He, then, speak to us betimes? Does He reveal the attitude of His mind and will and spirit towards us? Does He confirm to us the Christ-concept of Himself as "Our Father"? The answer to that is the answer of human experience. Let me give you an instance from my own ministry.

I had spent a busy day and was returned home in the evening when I was asked if I had called at a certain home, where dwelt a widowed woman with her two sons. Having spent the day in an opposite section of my pastoral field, I answered in the negative.

Following my negative reply, "Did you know that this afternoon George hanged himself in their barn?" I was asked.

This was the youngest of the two boys, a boy who had spent the evening before in our home with a group of young people gathered there for a social programme, and he the happiest and merriest amongst them all. New this boy, he was but fifteen years of age, was dead, the victim of his own reckless folly. His days of service in Christian undertakings, or in servitude to sin, were ended, and his last act —was it, could it be—a crime, the consequence of which must be the committal of his soul forever into the abyss of an eternal Hades?

I immediately re-harnessed the horse and drove to that home, impressed with the significance of such an untoward circumstance upon the heart of his mother. That boy, doubtless, had been the subject of her many prayers and the object of her Christian hope. Now he was taken away and under circumstances which made it impossible for her to believe, if the teachings and the dogmas of the time were true, that her prayers had been answered, or her hope for his salvation realized.

On my arrival at the place, I discovered the yard full of vehicles and people, and the house overflowing with the concourse of women who had gathered there from all the surrounding countryside. When I drew near to the door, I could hear a hysterical cry, the piercing wail of the mother,

"Is my boy, my George, lost?"

That was the question also which that concourse of people were asking amongst themselves, as they listened to the woman's wailing, agonizing cries. To that question there was one of them who had a ready and positive and an assured answer, a woman whose fervency in respect to her Christian hope was well known, and whose good deeds also among them had not been a few:

"Of course he's lost. The Bible says that no murderer shall enter into the kingdom of heaven, and he is guilty of murder, self-murder, the worst kind of murder."

Declarations such as these, though they were quite in harmony with the teachings of the time, relieved nothing of the distress of that bereaved mother's spirit Instead, they aided in increasing the burden of her already over-burdened, despairing and fearful heart.

When I was entered into the house, I observed the mother lying on a couch, dressed as she had been when she went out and discovered that gruesome spectacle, the spectacle of her son's lifeless body suspended by a rope from one of the beams of the barn, at the sight of which she fell down paralyzed, coming to consciousness only to experience all the distressing consequences which flow from such a tragic incident of life.

When word had been passed to her that I was in the room, she ceased her walls and her calls for the time and waited in quietude for my approach to her immediate presence. Standing by her side, she grasped my proffered hand in both of hers, and in a tone of voice which I shall never forget, she repeated the question which she had been calling out all afternoon,

Is my boy, my George, lost?"

What answer should I give her? What answer could I give her?

Judged by outward appearance, this boy was guilty of a great and abhorrent crime. He was young, it is true, but on the other hand, he was old enough to know right from wrong. He was sufficiently schooled and experienced to know that man's supreme duty in life is to eschew that which is evil and cleave to that which is good. He was not, however, old enough, nor schooled enough, to realize what effect that crime was going to have on his mother's destiny as well as on his own, if the God which brought him into being were such a God as the Christendom of the day believed him to be.

In this instance, as in all circumstances of life, the responsibility of this act of folly and wrong-doing could not be charged wholly against the boy. His life was a part of a long past, and that past, in accord with the judgment of his grandmother, had something to do in making this tragedy now a part of his own and his mother's life. When the body was discovered, a messenger was sent to a neighbouring city, where she lived, and she was told that an accident had happened and that he was dead. Instantly and eagerly she enquired,

"Did he commit suicide?"

When the answer was given in the affirmative, in a tone of stoic fatalism, she offered the explanation,

"There never has been a generation of that family (her own husband's family), without a suicide."

Here was a youth, who as yet was only on the threshold of life, a boy possessing his own potentiality, and the individuality and responsibility arising from that potentiality; yet, a boy who was also a part of a system which produced suicides seasonally; belonging to a family of which the committing of suicide was a characteristic trait; and since he had not fought against that fatal tendency inherited from a long line of his ancestors, but had permitted himself to follow in their footsteps, therefore, according to the dogma and teachings of the time, he was doomed to spend an eternity of years in agonizing torment in the abyss prepared for those guilty of such reckless folly.

But the mother's heart would not have it so. True, she knew these dogmas; knew they were proclaimed every Sabbath from many pulpits in many lands; knew the claim made that God was behind them to enforce them. But now, for the first time in her own history, she was up against the application of them, an application which sentenced a member of her household to the harsh and cruel destiny which they claimed would be of such criminals as he. Yet, notwithstanding the positive confidence with which her teachers taught these dogmas, her heart said,

"Surely these do not apply to my son? "

Did she put this as a question to the new-thought schoolmen of to-day, they would have answered,

"Assuredly not. God is 'Our Father,' a God so perfect in His love, so forgiving in His spirit, and so compassionate in His mercy that none needing His aid will be turned away empty; and, 'blessed is he who trusteth in Him.'"

Not to the schoolmen though, but to me, as the minister, was this question brought for answer. The responsibility to answer was mine. I must give judgment upon it. There was no escape. But the mother did not know, neither did the concourse of people know, the significance of that question. Not only was she asking me to unveil the doings of the other world, and to tell her what reception her son had received from

Him who inhabiteth eternity, but if the unity and solidarity of the human family is a reality of our earthly existence she was asking me to tell what reception at death would the whole of the human family receive at His hands. She was asking me to answer a question which philosophers and sages have been grappling with for ages and yet haven't produced an answer which has received the unanimous assent of mankind. She was asking me to answer the question whether tragedy or triumph was to be the issue of all human life? Whether it was to be the conquest of wrong over right, or right over wrong? The conquest of falsehood over truth, or truth over falsehood? Whether the human family was to suffer a great division, one section destined to the doom of an eternal Hades, but the other to enter into the bliss of an eternal Paradise? The one to receive a just punishment for the ill-deserts of their lives, but the others to receive a divine favour which they did not merit? This was the question which she had set for me, the great question, the question of the destiny of the human family.

Was it because from my earliest infancy I had been schooled in the teachings of One who said, "When ye pray, say, 'Our Father'"? Or was it because the Spirit of God spake, using me as His instrument? Or was it because both of us, in honouring the Christ-concept of God, were honouring God? Whatever the producing cause, my answer was the answer which the new-thought schoolmen would have given had they been in my circumstances, though in my remotest thought I had not associated myself with that movement, that is to say, consciously. I found myself in a set of circumstances which compelled me, *nolens volens*, to be in obedience to the Scriptural counsel, "Take no thought what ye shall speak." Pre-thought, or after-thought, there was none, for there could not be. I spake as my concept of God and my faith bade me speak. Had I a different faith, my answer, doubtless, would have been different.

At any rate, believing that God was a Father, perfect in His love, possessing in perfect fullness a forgiving spirit, and exercising towards us a compassionate mercy, all-powerful, I answered her in accord with that concept. There could be no hedging around the problem, nor any falling back on extenuating circumstances concerning which I knew nothing. Drawing her attention to her own affectionate regard for her son, and the impossibility that she could sentence him to such a doom, no matter what of wrong-doing she might bring up as a charge against him, I directed her thought upon those three attributes found in the heart of "Our Father."

"God will not do against George, your son, what you could not do against him in alike circumstances yourself."

That was my answer.

The women in that packed room were waiting with a stillness which could be felt, alert in ear, to hear what my answer would be. It was more than curiosity, this. Brought face to face with one of those occasions in life which speak of destiny, they waited with hopeful hearts for an answer which would give respite to that mother's fears, and bring some measure of comfort to her heart. Had I the answer which could do this?

Certainly the concept of God with a sword in His hand and anger in His heart could not. Considered from the viewpoint of the mother, fear had taken possession of her spirit and it was shaking her soul with torturing violence; and it was there because that the concept of God, handed down through the ages, had put it there. Could this fear be removed from its place of entrenchment, it could only be by the production of another concept of God, a concept different, and one which would meet also the requirements of salvation for her son.

Had I not a more enlightened and a more humane concept, had not Christ taught us that God was "Our Father," had not my parents passed this teaching along to me, I would have been shut up to that old, time-worn, Pagan concept of God, for it was from the Pagan world we received it, and I would be under the necessity of either evading the question, or inventing some subterfuge, to escape the issue. But the Christ-concept of God as "Our Father," solved the problem for both the mother and her son; the concept of a God providing love where love was needed, forgiveness where forgiveness was needed, showing mercy where mercy was needed. What better concept of God

45

could we have than that? What, and since it came from Christ, truer one? I drew that mother's attention to that concept, and the spirit of God did the rest.

Immediately the word was passed along through the crowd that I had said to the mother that her son was saved. But that was not my statement. It was the deduction of their own thinking from what I had said. But their deduction was right, for that is the only conclusion which could be deduced logically from the Christ-concept of God as "Our Father." If God had, as I was trying to get that mother to believe, a love equal to that of hers, a spirit of forgiveness equal to hers, a spirit of pitying mercy equal to hers, such love and forgiveness and mercy as she, his mother, would exercise towards her own child, then there could not be for her son, the committal of his soul to a place of eternal torment.

Not only did God possess these attributes in equal degree to hers, but His so far transcended hers, that what she held in imperfect degree, he held in perfect.

It would be impossible, then, that a God of such love, having so forgiving a spirit, and with such a pitying mercy, do anything other than exercise forgiveness towards that son and his sin.

But there was another aspect in this untoward circumstance which escaped the observation and appreciation of both the mother and the people gathered there; this, that the fate of the son must of necessity be the fate of the mother also. If being saved means happiness for the saved one, then unless the son also, the mother could not be saved. How could that mother be happy in heaven, if her son was suffering agonizing torment, misery and discomfort in the abyss of Hades, as the doctrine of the time taught that he would be? It is absurd to speak of the mother in a state of rapturous bliss, while all the while she is consciously aware that her son, whom she loves, and in whose well-being she has an interest equal to her own, is living in a state of eternal torment and misery.

When that son was born, he became a part, an inseparable part, of her life. There was a oneness between them created which never could be taken away. As long as the love she bore him continued, so long would she suffer when he suffered, be glad when he was glad, and sorrowful when he was sorrowful. There is no way by which that relationship could be taken away, except by both ceasing to exist.

So also, "Our Father." The happiness of God is bound up in, and made dependent upon, the happiness of his children. The shepherd is not content as long as even the tiniest lamb is out, "lost" in the wilderness.

Here, then, was a perplexing problem of human life, which the one concept of God did not and could not solve, but which the other did. The one made the perplexity still more perplexing; the other removed the perplexity by solving the problem.

Any concept, unless it commends itself to our reason cannot command our faith. Neither will it receive universal assent unless it meets the needs and the requirements of the human family. The doctrine of the reprobate lost, and the division of the human family into saved and lost, did not meet the soul needs of this widowed mother, bereft of her son through no fault of hers, but by an act of self-destruction on the part of her son which would place him in the category of the lost, in accord with the old-time concept of God. But accepting the Christ-concept of God, and making her son the recipient of that love and forgiveness and mercy of "Our Father," notwithstanding the wrong-doing which he did, and you have a concept which meets the requirements of this incident and every similar incident in human life.

Continue on in this old-thought concept of God, and in the belief of a reprobate lost, and you make of life a great tragedy, and that not only for this earthly life, but for that life continued on throughout the long aeons of an endless future. Replace this former concept of God by the one taught by the Great Teacher of Nazareth, and you have an ideal of God which gives to the human soul an inspired faith to noble living, a thought of Him which supplies a solution to many of the now perplexing problems of life and gives to all of mankind a foundation for an assured hope bringing aspiration to the living and peace of mind to the dying.

If, however, the first concept of God, which has come down to us through the Ages, is true, if the picture of God with an angry countenance and a drawn sword, is the reality which the dying sinner has to face at death, if the doctrine of a reprobate lost stands, then you make of life a great and inexcusable tragedy, and you create for mankind a destiny in which the greatest good that could come to man would be, as a certain noted pessimist declared, "never to have been born at all, and the next best to it, to die young."

This viewpoint of Schopenhauer receives its answer in the idea of the Soul of God released by Christ and embodied in the faith and hope of present-day, enlightened Christianity; an idea which predicates of Him not Only the attribute of love, but a love so full and complete, so perfect, that no element of wrath, anger, or even provocation can find a place to create a disturbing relationship of His mind to any one member of the human family. To see the derelict restored and made whole, the degraded one lifted up from the pit into which he had fallen, the sinful forgiven and the rebel shown mercy: to have a vision of the whole of mankind, not one excepted, moving forward in a united, organic whole, to a goal that is good, this is the Hope to which the Christ-concept of God directs the faith of the world, and it is the one, we verily believe, which has the backing of truth and God behind it.

THE POTENTIALITY AND
THE NATURE OF MAN

THE "DESTINY OF MAN" is dependent upon two things, first the nature of God; and, second, the nature of man; that is to say, it is dependent upon the Soul of God and the potentiality of Man. In a sense, since man is God's creation, the "Destiny of Man" may therefore be said to be wholly dependent upon God.

The concept of the Soul of God which we have received from the teachings of Christ, from this the New-thought schoolmen draw the Conclusion that the division of the human family into "saved" and "lost," one section of them destined for paradise, but the other section for Gehenna, while both of them are equally the children of the one God and Father, that such a concept of the "Destiny of Man cannot be maintained. To cause such a division to exist would be to predicate disharmony and discord in the social order, while all that we know or believe of God leads us to the thought that He is a lover of harmony and concord, a lover of beauty, and things beautiful; a lover of all things good and true; and that He has carried out the creation of man in accord with this law of harmony and concord.

The phrase, "The good, the beautiful and the true," was in much use at one time by public speakers and writers, to express the sum total of all the realities of our known universe; if not all, then the most important parts of it. In the thoughts of mankind, the "beautiful has not, perhaps, received the consideration which has been given to the other two. Nevertheless, "beauty" is a very important reality of our life, and has very much to do in creating that happiness and joy, without which life would be for us a very drab affair indeed. As a component part of the true soul of a good man it occupies a very prominent place.

Tastes differ in respect to what is beautiful as well as in regard to other things. One will turn to nature, and its varied scenery in search of that which is beautiful. Another will find the beautiful in some achievement of man.

Four times in my experience has an admiration of the beautiful been stirred up within me to an unusual degree by some incident in the objective world without, brought within the range of my knowledge through the sense of sight.

Looking over from the escarpment upon which I stood at the foot of Brock's monument, Niagara Peninsula, Ontario, there I beheld a valley extending eastward towards Lake Erie, and watered by the Niagara River, a scene of beauty which is perhaps second to no other of its kind in the world, when seen at a particular time of the year, and under favourable sunlight conditions. Dotted with well laid-out vineyards and farm houses, in the creation of which landscape architecture had been generously utilized, one could not but feel that there Nature and man had entered into co-partnership to create in the scene before me, one of the most beautiful things in the world.

On another occasion, standing at the top of the Turtle Mountains, Southern Manitoba, one evening in September, there was spread out before my view what appeared to be one large harvest-field, but, instead, the acreage of one farmer joining with the acreage of another. The sun was dipping down below the western horizon, throwing its beams of falling light on this vast wheat— acreage, and giving to the waving grain that hue of golden yellow which artists would like to reproduce but cannot. Twelve binders, each drawn by two pairs of horse-teams, were at work in this large field. A sense of the beautiful, associated with the feeling of a great plenty, obsessed me for the moment. Here again was the co-partnership of man and Nature in the creation of an achievement, beautiful.

A third view, more entrancing and thrilling than either of these two, it was my privilege one day to discover quite unexpectedly. Riding over the prairies on an early June morning, all at once I came within view for the first time of one of the poet's "gardens of the desert." Reining up my bronco to a full stop, I sat thrilled with a sense of the beautiful in the scene before me. The prairie, as far as eye could see, was transfigured into one great flower garden. The glory of Solomon was outshone a millionfold. The hand of man was not there. What a lavish expenditure of beauty, if not created for the enjoyment of the Creator himself.

While all of these were magnificent creations of beauty, the most beautiful thing in the world, this, I did not discover in any one of these three things. That most beautiful thing, to me, was discovered one day lying upon its mother's knee. Its morning bath had just been finished; its hair lay in promiscuous curls beyond its forehead; its deep blue eyes sparkled with the enjoyment of a great delight. It was waving its hands and kicking its feet, and cooing, its first efforts to achieve a language. All these activities were the expressions of a great joy from having in its possession the gift of life. The most beautiful thing in the world, because it was so created by it was also, and at the same time, the greatest and best of all his created beings.

In my admiration of that babe, I said to the mother, "What is this that you have there on your lap?"

"This," she answered, and there was the expression of a great admiration on her countenance as she looked down upon it, "This, is a gift from God."

The mother was right. Yet, already and before that babe has had time to do either good or bad, her little gift is slandered from two quarters. It is slandered, first, by a certain section of organized Christianity.

"Do you know," say—they, "that, notwithstanding the outward appearance of beauty, deep down in the nature of that child, there is planted an element of discord, an element of depravity, and unless there comes a miracle of grace into that child's life which will eliminate that depravity, the home-goal of its destiny is Gehenna."

Instead, then, of looking upon this babe as a marvellous creation of beauty, there is the concept of an element of ugliness, of deformity, of depravity in its nature, placed there by its Creator, and this believed not by an occasional person here and there, but the only thought-idea which has been held by many generations of mankind for centuries who verily believed that this idea was nothing other than the truth concerning the nature of that babe, and every unit of the human family.

To-day, however, there is a growing representation of the human family who have a different thought-idea. One of these looking at the babe ventures her contrary judgment.

"I have read somewhere, that a human babe is created in the image of God, and as I look at that cooing, happy face on your lap, I verily believe it."

She has read "somewhere." That somewhere was the Holy Scriptures. Of course, if the verity of these sacred writings be denied, it their statements concerning the teachings of Christ are not believed, then there is no other source to which we can turn to know the truth which God and Christ have taught us. To those who believe that the Bible is a safe guide in this, as in all other matters, and that it discovers faithfully for us the deep things concerning our own nature and God's, seeing that babe is believing that it, and every new unit of the human race, is born into the image of God, created in His likeness.

"Let us make man in our image, after our likeness": said God at the beginning of time. "So God created man in His own image, in the image of God created be them."

If this passage of the Scriptures be taken as recording a fact in respect to the creation of man, then to the claim that man was born into the world with an element of depravity implanted in his nature, an element of deformity, discord and disharmony, there could be but one answer, "It is not so."

To those who would add an element of depravity to the spirit life of the child, which is not there, and thus sully the reputation of the child in respect to its beauty, we must add as the second of the babe's slanderers, those who would withdraw from that child the right to be called "a gift from God." I have before me an article written by a certain Doctor Blacker, teacher, magazine writer, and physicist, informing us through the columns of a New York; magazine that since 1875, no one views the human babe as "a gift from God."

The present-day school of Christian thinkers will not admit this statement of Doctor Blacker. They assert that the divine origin of the human babe is believed and held with firmer conviction to-day than at any other time previous to this in the history of Christendom, and that because of a fuller and more intelligible concept of what that babe discovers itself to be when first it comes under the notice of human observation.

Shall the scientist look for the origin of that babe in the material universe? Look? Looking alone will never discover the truth concerning it. Reason and faith must be added to observation. The origin of the babe lies beyond the realm of the hearing ear and the seeing eye; far beyond the realm of the merely physical. Deep down in the realm of the spiritual, there and there only, shall we be able to obtain the answer to the question from whence it came.

Beautiful as it is in its outward appearance, there is something grander and more glorious there than that which can be observed by the ordinary intellectual faculties of man. Mortal eye cannot discover it, but to the eye of faith and reason it is seen to be of all the sentient beings of God's created works, not only the most beautiful, but the most wonderful and miraculous, so miraculous in its conception that it staggers the power of the human mind to comprehend it.

Into that handiwork of God, for it is God's creation, there is something which God has placed there to make it the greatest of all of his creations. That something is His own likeness, His own spirit. The spirit-life of man, He created an emanation of Himself. Intelligence was given to man, and gifts and endowments as inherent powers of that intelligence. Hence man can think and plan, and design and purpose, and create, because the Father, of whom he is the offspring, thinks and plans and designs and purposes and creates.

But these powers He created in man first in potentiality— not yet being, nor yet becoming, but, having the power to be and become what his Father, designed and purposed he should be and become — this it is which determines for man both his nature and destiny.

When the physicist reached the atomic cell in his quest for the origin of man, he stopped and said, "There is the commencement of its life."

"Not so," Christian faith answers. "Even at that time in its career, it has had already a long history associated with its life, a history which, if written out in full, would take the whole life-time of any ordinary physicist to read, if he devoted all his time to this and nothing else. And even then he would not be able to tell the full story of its life, nor answer one-half of the questions which arise in connection with its origin."

"From whence came the colour of its eyes? In what storehouse did God keep the pigment all these aeons while waiting for the time to arrive for the creation of this atom? Why did that babe go back three generations for the colour of its hair?"

These and thousands of other questions have been asked and yet no scientist has been able to answer any one of them, because here we are dealing with matters concerning which we can only believe; cannot know. Here, as the Scriptures express it, we walk by faith, not by sight.

Events, occurrences, occasions and circumstances may arise to confirm us in our faith or to cause an element of doubt to come into our mind concerning our faith, but if we are to have any assurance in respect to the origin of each unit of the human family that assurance can only come to us through faith.

But here again knowledge comes to the aid of our faith, both working together to ascertain the truth concerning the origin of human life; and, from this co-partnership, we come to certainty concerning ourselves and every new unit of the race.

"It is true," say the new-thought schoolmen, "that man possesses a nature-life, and that this nature-life begins its career a product of nature; and that it is put in subjection to the laws of nature for its preservation and growth. Yet in addition to this, it has a spirit-life, this part of its being, created in the image of God, a part in which there is no element of disharmony, deformity, or depravity to be found."

In accord with this concept the new-thought school—men make this further pronouncement, "That man is born a potentiality to become perfect, even as perfect as God would have him be, and that each member of the human family will realize his potentiality, not one excepted."

LIFE'S CERTAINTIES

THE FIRST AND premier law of human life, the one under which it is first placed in subjection, is the law of growth. "Thou shalt grow." This is a command of nature, and there is no alternative other than the obedience to it. Should anything intervene or arise to prevent obedience to this law, what then? There is no life, that is all. Where there is life there will be growth, and where there is no growth, life ceases to be.

If a life is made to grow there must be some end, some goal unto which it is to grow.

When a new unit of the human family is born into this world, his first requirement is the supply of energy, or rather energies, by means of which he will be able to carry out the requirements of this law. He will need energy from the sun; he cannot live without heat and light; energy from the clouds, he cannot live without something to drink; energy from the air, he cannot live without oxygen; products of the soil must also be sent to him, he cannot live without food.

For all of these things, he cannot make provision himself; neither his parents. The making of the necessary provision for obedience to this law is beyond the power of both of them. Yet when the occasion arises the provision is made. By whom was that provision made, if not by the One who ordained the law and placed human life in subjection under it? Undoubtedly, it is the Creator of the law who makes provision for its obedience, and supplies every need to this end, not only in the days of his helpless infancy, but throughout his whole life as well. The need is the guarantee of its fulfillment.

Here, then, we find a law, and for that law a universe created where provision is made for supplying all the requirements necessary that obedience to that law may be carried out. Has this law a purpose? Is there a definite goal as the end of its aim? Thou shalt grow, but unto what?

In the challenge of Christ to the world, "Be ye perfect, even as your heavenly Father is perfect," we have both his concept of the destiny of man and his concept of the of all human endeavour.

Could we have a complete compendium of all of the concepts which Jesus released and taught concerning God, concerning the nature of man, concerning the family, and concerning the destiny of man, we would have a complete body of Christian truth, a complete syllabus of all the required articles of the Christian faith. In respect to the teachings of Christ, it is by faith alone we can be assured that the things which he has declared to us are true, for he speaks of the things with which faith alone has to do; the things which are outside of the realm of knowledge.

Among the things with which faith alone has to the to-morrow of our lives is one of the most important. Concerning this, the first thought which is borne home to our minds is, that while God has given us faculties by means of which we can lay hold of the past and the present, He has given us no faculty by means of which we can descry and know the future. For the past, the faculty of memory is given, so that by it we can take the things of yesterday and set them before our mind for the use of to-day. Printing and writing comes to the aid of this faculty so that by means of these inventions we are able to keep a record of past and notable events. In this way our knowledge of yesterday can go back thousands of years.

In regard to the present, we have our senses, seeing, hearing, smelling, all these gates of knowledge which tell us of what is going on at present. But there is no power given to anyone by God which will enable him to say with certainty what is going to happen on the morrow. Here we walk by faith, not by sight.

Had we no faith, the whole of to-morrow would he to us a closed book. But this power visualizes the to-morrow of our lives. It lays plans on the basis of this vision. It carries out projects on the strength of it. It assays great undertakings and achieves them. Without faith these things would be impossible to us.

What is the origin of this faith? From whence does it come? The only satisfying answer to this question is, that it is a part of our spirit-life; an inherent power of that life. We are created, not in supposition, nor in theory, but in actual fact, in the likeness of God. Our spirit-life is like His in everything but one thing. We are not perfect. But we are imperfect not to remain imperfect. So Christ, His great messenger to the world, challenges us to achieve our destiny: "Be ye perfect, even as your heavenly Father is perfect." There is the goal set for man for his achievement and attainment. This challenge of Christ carries with it the presupposition that is the greatest of all of our heritages, since it is in that to-morrow wherein lies the achievement of our destined goal.

As we cast our thoughts forward into the to-morrow of our lives, we face both certainties and uncertainties. This may be illustrated by the leaves on a tree. "Leaves die in their season." This is the law which insures the life of these leaves to continue until the coming autumn. It is certain that practically all of the leaves of the tree will live on until then, and that they will all die with the first coming of frost, the first fall of snow in winter. While of all of them, and in a general way, this will be true, of individual leaves it may not be so. Some may be withered by a mildew almost as soon as they have come out of their bud; others may be gnawed off their branches by worms; while still others may be nipped and fall off because of an early summer's frost. Though, then, we can say of leaves in general, that they die "in their season," we cannot say this of all without exception.

There are some things uncertain in the to-morrow of our lives. To-morrow's sun will shine the same as to-day's, but will we be there—to see it shine? To-morrow's call to duty will be as strong as today's, but will we be as strong to obey that call? Seed-time and harvest will come next year, but will it come to every farmer, or even to every nation of the world?

In the to-morrow of our lives, there are, without doubt, uncertainties; yet, on the other hand there are some things which are fixed and certain and must take place. Two things, at least, there are upon which we can base a certain faith and there will be no miscarriage. Concerning God and His laws, these abideth ever; they change not. These are they which give to our future its hope and its certainty.

As we scan the future, knowing that therein will be both certainties and uncertainties, things fixed and things unstable, things unchangeable and things changeable, in which of these two categories shall we place the destiny of man? Shall we say that it, at least, belongs to the things which are fixed, stable and unchangeable? As Christ gave expression to his challenge, his thought, without doubt, would reflect back to that ancient record concerning the creation of man at the beginning of time.

"And God said, Let us make man in our image, after our likeness." "So God created man in His own image; in the image of God created he him."

If God created man in His own likeness, made man in his spirit-life an emanation of His own spirit, giving to that emanation the power to become perfect, wherein lies the possibility of that life ending in tortured ruin, in endless tragedy? If this concept be sustained and that, in veritable fact, man is in his spirit-life an emanation of then such an ending to his life would appear to our thinking, impossible.

Hitherto, the churches have taught that in the destiny of man, we have one at the most uncertain of all the uncertainties of life. Of course there would have to be this uncertainty about it, if the viewpoint of a divided destiny for mankind were the correct one. If the human family had to suffer division, one division destined to a goal of good, and the other division fated to meet an evil end; the one division losing out because of the demerit of their lives, but the other division winning out because of a special favour granted to them from heaven, with the reason for their division thus made wholly arbitrary, it could not but be that there would be the greatest of uncertainty as to which ones should win out and which ones fail.

From this challenge of Christ, we are forced to the conclusion that the support of the Teacher of Nazareth is on the side of the new-thought, rather than upon the side of the old-thought schoolmen. Attached to this challenge of Christ are certain pre-suppositions which would make the destiny of man a fixed and unchangeable thing if the challenge is to be anything other than a meaningless proclamation.

If we accept the Christian idea of the origin of man, we discover the first stage in his career to be an idea in the mind of God, and that God had a design, a purpose in creating him. This design, or purpose, is disclosed in the next stage of his career, the stage in which he is not yet being, nor yet becoming, but having the power to be and become that which God designs he shall become; in other words, a potentiality unrealized, and thus created by God from set design and purpose. All this being accounted true, from this we can deduce no other conclusion than that man shall in due time realize his potentiality. We cannot conceive of God making pattern and design merely to amuse himself. The design, the pattern, we take it, is created with the definite purpose in the mind of God that it shall be realized.

A half-century ago, a certain Reverend Doctor Thomas of Liverpool, Eng., was on a lecture tour throughout Wales. At the close of one of his lectures in a Welsh village, a youth, seventeen years of age, rose up and moved a vote of thanks to the speaker for his lecture. The high order of the youth's abilities, and the excellencies of his speech so impressed Doctor Thomas that he wrote a paragraph and sent it the next day to one of the Welsh weeklies under the caption, "I have discovered a man." What Doctor Thomas discovered was not a man, but a youth seventeen years of age with all the rawness of youthful thought in his speech; but in this youth he saw the promise, the potentiality of the man who was yet to be. The youth, in the person of the Honourable Lloyd George, a premier parliamentarian of Great Britain, a world-figure in the great holocaust of 1914—to 1918, has since then become what Doctor Thomas saw and prophesied he would become.

Not an occasional one, but every unit of the human family bears in his person the image and design and purpose of the God who created him. This challenge of Christ pre-supposes the fulfillment of every potentiality; pre-supposes that there can be no miscarriage nor failure in the design and purpose of God with regard to even one man. If there cannot, if every man is created a potentiality, if every potentiality is divinely purposed to be realized, then the destiny of man is no longer an uncertainty, but one of the fixed and unchangeable certainties of the to-morrow of our lives. How many circumstances might have arisen from the time that Doctor Thomas first came in contact with the youth Lloyd George and observed his potentiality until the time that the great world war broke out, any: one of which could have prevented him from realizing his potentiality. That they did not come is due to the fact that He who designed the potentiality, designed and purposed also the means, the agencies, the protective forces which would guarantee its realization.

Many potentialities are not realized, we are told, and many others are misdirected. All men do not make a proper use of their gifts and their endowments. Some men go so far as to make a wicked and criminal use of them. Shall not these suffer in accord with the old-thought school, because of this? Even the sayings of Christ have been quoted in support of the likelihood of this.

On the first day of the passion week, as He made his way in triumphal procession to Jerusalem, one incident of memorable import is recorded in that day's proceedings. When the procession had reached the brow of the hill, and the acclaim was at its highest, at the place where the road begins to clip downward, Jesus paused. He cast his eyes over and viewed the brow of the next hill immediately before him. There on that hill was the city of David, and, centrally situated, the temple, where God was wont, in days of yore, to meet with His people in worship. In vision Jesus saw the end of the city and its temple service, the doom of the people and their city because of their attitude to truth and to God. The tears streamed down his cheeks and in lamentation he gave vent to the heart-hunger of God for His people as he beheld the multitude trampling this opportunity for enlightenment under their feet.

"Would that you had known, while yet there was time, even you, the things that make for peace! But now they have been hidden from your sight."

What was it that Jesus saw in vision before him, which caused this outburst of sorrow? Was it the end of their national life? Or was it the end of their spirit—life? We say of the spirit-life that it is indestructible because it is an emanation of God's; but, the property of indestructibility cannot be said to belong inherently to the nation's life. Hence we conclude that it was the end of the Davidic kingdom over which Jesus wept on that occasion. The nation perished that the individuals comprising the nation might be saved.

If mal-growths and misdirected gifts are exemplified in the history of a human life, then we may expect corrective forces to be at work in the world to bring about a recovery in their lives. Otherwise there will be miscarriages and failures and endless uncertainties in respect to human destinies. If the fifth axiom of the new-thought schoolmen, "That man is born a potentiality to become perfect, even as perfect as God would have him be, and that, each member of the human family will realize his potentiality, not one excepted," if this is to be an axiom of truth in veritable fact, then a recovery of these lives from the wrong course which they are following must take place and a new direction given to the use made of their endowments and gifts in ways which shall guarantee that there shall be an achievement of their potentiality, and that for every one of them.

We have a graphic illustration of the prophecy of this in the attitude of Christ to little children. Looking at their young lives, and seeing the possibilities of evil as well as of good in these, he gathered them to himself, promising them the protection of heaven. It cannot be that any of these little ones shall be allowed to grow up only to perish. "For," he said, "of such is the Kingdom of heaven." This could not be unless they were "such" in the purposed and planned realization of God creating such a universe that all things should be made to work together to insure them a perpetual place in that Kingdom.

But Christ goes further than to prophesy for them a place in the Kingdom. He proceeds to name the one great agency provided to insure the realization of it. This is nothing other than the power inherent in man himself. Man created in the image of God, his spirit-life, an emanation of God's, this spirit inherent in every man, will be energized by a further enduement of the same spirit, and as a result recovery will come where recovery is needed. Growth, advance, progress will be made in every life until the challenge of Christ is realized by every life, not one excepted. Of this work of the spirit, we have ample illustrations. Suffice it to mention one.

When slavery was at its height, there lived in England a young man, who grew up to love drink and the dance hall and all the evils associated with these two things. As a young man he could not see any evil in them, as the votaries of these things see no evil in them to-day. But the spirit of God dwelling within him from his earliest infancy began to draw his attention to his life, to its uselessness and sinfulness. It showed him life, in another, but truer, aspect. His eyes became opened; he surrendered himself to the call of righteousness and of service, unto which the Spirit of God had directed and inspired him. What significance had all this? What but that the purpose and design which God had in raising him up should be realized. All around him was the fierce and cruel traffic in human beings, the stealing of men, women and children from their homes their shipment to the United States, and the sale of them there to be goaded to a service fitted only for cattle.

Inspired by God's appointed Energizer within and about him, he was stirred up to seek redress for the helpless victims of this criminal evil. He lifted his voice against it. He went among his old cronies of the drinking brothel and called upon them to organize themselves against it. He spent night and day calling upon men to root it out. Soon everywhere people joined up with him. The government was petitioned. All classes stood shoulder to shoulder with him in his effort to end this deadly and cruel evil. Would this evil be thus and so soon ended if his recovery stood outside of the possibilities of achievement within the scope of the energizing work of the Holy Spirit of God? The name of Wilberforce stands out to-day on the pages of history as one of England's greatest welfare workers, because man can be, and is recovered from service and slavery to evil through this energizing work of the agencies of God, created for the recovery and renewal of man.

But recovery does not take place in the case of every one, at least to outward appearance it does not, on this side of the grave. Many instances there are of persons who have lived their whole lives upon the earth, making a wrongful use of their gifts right to the end; a misdirected life, and unrealized potentiality. In respect to these, they will have to be brought under subjection to the laws of their being, subsequently. Hence we predicate the immortality of the soul, not only for these, but for all mankind, a continuance of life, in order that, for these, their recovery may be brought about; and that, for all mankind, their potentiality shall be realized and the goal of their destiny achieved. Imperfect we were born; imperfect we die. The challenge of Christ to be realized for even one person, pre-supposes then the continuance of the soul after death. Hence we have the seventh axiom of the new-thought schoolmen, "That when a man dies, the disintegration of his nature-life does not affect his spirit-life; that after death there is an unbroken continuance of his spirit-life under conditions suited to the carrying out of the realization of his potentiality; that he will continue to move forward from stage to stage in progress, until he has achieved the goal set for man, "Be ye perfect, even as your heavenly Father is perfect."

Lead on, O God, our Father,
Thy words of truth are dear;
There is no other leading,
Thy voice alone we hear;
We hear Thy gracious speaking;
We hear Thy trumpet call;
And now, O God, our Father,
To thee we give our all.

We come, O God, our Father,
We come with thankful heart;
Thy promise of redemption,
From it we'll ne'er depart;
We'll cling to God, our Father,
We'll trust his promised word;
And with our fellow-trav'llers
We'll live in sweet accord.

Lead on, O God, our Father,
Thy call we now shall hear;
In tumult of Life's conflict
Be Thou forever near;
Through days of dark despairing,
Through nights foreboding doom,
Thy Presence ever near us
Shall banish all life's gloom.

CONVERSION BY SPIRITUAL RENEWAL THROUGH GROWTH

THE DARKNESS OF night had settled down on the hillside grove of Bethany, where Jesus, as was His wont, had retired with His disciples that he might with them spend the evening in restful quietude. But it was not to be. Though the day have been one of excessive toil, a further service was required of Him.

Out of the darkness there emerged a member of the Jewish Sanhedrin, puzzled in mind concerning the approach of the Kingdom of God, but confident in Jesus that he was a teacher sent from God to give the needed instruction concerning the Kingdom – its nature, its approach, and the benefits it would confer on the Jewish people when it did come. He introduced himself by saying, "We know that thou art a teacher sent from God." In this estimate of Jesus he was in marked contrast to the rest of his class, who looked upon Jesus, not even as a prophet, but as an out-and-out impostor. Jesus, glad of a new opportunity of service, proceeded to enlighten this Pharisee, whose name was Nicodemus, concerning the Kingdom and the relationship of all of mankind in respect to it.

As the vision of the things which were to be was presented, the difficulties which stood in the way of their fulfilment along the lines indicated by Jesus, seemed to the cultured mind of this Israelite, insurmountable, yes, even physically impossible.

"How can these things be?" he exclaimed incredulously.

Especially was he puzzled concerning the required conditions necessary on the part of each individual to become a member of God's Kingdom.

"Must the processes of nature be repeated and man become re-born?"

The answer of Jesus was not in respect to man's nature-life, but his spirit-life, and the spiritual powers and processes at work to effect the required conditions.

"Except a man be born of water and the spirit, he cannot see the Kingdom of God."

Years after, a summarized statement concerning what he had heard that night was written by the beloved apostle, who, along with the other eleven disciples, had been listening in to the conversation. This he incorporated into his Gospel, a record which has become since, in the esteem of many Bible students, one of the most important passages in the sacred word. Certain statements of Nicodemus and of Jesus had riveted themselves upon his memory. These, the interjections of the one and the explanations of the other, he included in his record adding his own comments to which he attached that passage, informing us of the motivating influence which inspired all this Creative work on the part of God:

"For God so loved the world, that He gave His only begotten Son, that whosoever believeth in Him should not perish, but have everlasting life."

To the importance of this passage my own attention was called in early life. Emerging from youth to manhood, there was placed in my hand a book entitled "Grace and Truth." It was written by a clergyman of Glasgow, Scotland, named MacKay, a missionary to the sailors at that port, a book which at that time was able to command the interest of a large circle of readers, and still does. There was one chapter in the book which arrested my attention especially. It was his exposition of this passage in the Scriptures which comprised the record relating to the interview between Nicodemus and Jesus. Mr. MacKay singled out one passage of that recorded interview and made it the theme of his chapter:

"Except a man be born again, he cannot see the Kingdom of God."

The meaning which he attached to the word "again," in the quoted passage, was the then commonly accepted one, "a second time." Overlooking the fact that the translators could have chosen any one of four English words—"again," "anew," "from above," "in the beginning"—to express the meaning of the original Greek, he proceeded to build up his theory of conversion on the English word "again," as the proper word expressing the meaning of the Greek word.

At the time when this book was written, practically all of Christendom believed in the verbal inspiration of the Bible. This meant that no errors of any kind could creep into the Book; that it had the oversight of God in its composition, who not only gave the ideas to the writer, but the very words which he was to use. This oversight and protection from error was given also at the time when it became necessary to make translations from the original to some other language. There was no error, nor could there be, in the translated book, any more than there could be in the original. It would, at that time, be accounted heresy for anyone to even suggest: that the translators made any mistake in choosing the English word which they did, "again," to express the idea which the Greek word was meant to convey. So translated, this text was made to mean, Except a man be born a second time and another nature given to him, a new One, which would be free from the errors, the disabilities and the badness of the old, he is debarred from entering into the Kingdom of God."

This view of the nature of conversion pre-supposed depravity of nature on the part of man. It also made experience of conversion one of miraculous achievement with God as the author of the miracle. There was no place for obtaining the desired end by a process of renewal, or as a result of growth, in this concept of it. It was brought about in a moment of time by the exercise of a divine power, which not only created the new, but substituted this new creation in the place of the old in the personality of the one upon whom the miracle was performed.

Nothing," says this old school, "but a complete withdrawal of the old from existence and its replacement by something entirely new, would satisfy the requirements of a perfected human nature. The old must be discarded, annihilated, made to disappear, and the new must be brought in to replace it."

This, then, was the concept of the nature of man, the concept of salvation, and the concept of the method of obtaining that salvation to which I was first introduced by the reading of Mr. MacKay's book a short half-century ago, and there were no other concepts in vogue at that time, at least, none available to me. It was founded, as observed, on the doctrine of the depravity of human nature. The Sacred Writings were quoted in support of this doctrine, and texts were gathered here and there from out the Word, divorced from their context and set down as unassailable proofs of the truth of this depravity. There was no trend away from this teaching discernible at that time, but the great unanswered question remained unanswered:

"Why to some only were the benefits of this experience granted? Why were all others excluded?"

It was taken for granted by all that this was so, and there was nothing more to be said about it—the reason for its being so did not seriously matter.

When, then, a teaching began to introduce itself, a teaching which required the old-school to give up the divine fiat, and the divine miracle, in respect to conversion, a teaching which questioned the verbal inspiration of the Bible, a teaching which said that there was a possibility of emendations, interpolations, and even errors to creep into its text during the years in which it was coming down to us, then the old-school looked upon all those introducing or supporting such a teaching as emissaries of evil. It had the on many of these of making them more convinced than ever that theirs was the truth and that they were to do more than beware such a teaching; they must fight to destroy it.

But Mr. MacKay's book was not written for that purpose. It was written to bring the sailors of Glasgow to an acceptance of the Gospel story; to a faith in the message of saving truth brought to the world by the great Teacher of Nazareth. There was therefore no element of controversy introduced in it. It was a statement of what he believed to be the facts based on the traditional faith that the Bible came to us, as does our conversion, by divine word and divine miracle, the work wholly of an agency outside of man, and that a supernatural one. It was written for the purpose of making-disciples for the Kingdom at a time when as yet the influence of the teaching of renewal of man by process of growth through a power inherent in his own nature had not made its way into the church, at least, not to any appreciable extent.

Although I was much interested in the book, enjoyed the reading of it, it brought no new concept to my mind, no new experience into my life. The doctrines of the book, these were the teachings in which I was nurtured from my earliest infancy. Yet I am indebted to the book and to the reading of it for a valuable service which it rendered me, in the creation in my mind of the supreme value of that recorded interview by the Master of Nazareth with Nicodemus.

If there was anything of specially characteristic trait in the contents of the book, it was the profound emphasis which was placed on the depravity of human nature, the commonly accepted belief of that time—this, that man was created by God with an element of discord, disharmony, depravity implanted there as an inherent part of his life. This presupposition prevailed throughout the whole book, a universally believed article of the Christian faith of the time, a doctrine which subsequent study has discovered to be on a par with the flat earth, and a concept similar to the concept of the man who declares "there is no God,"—namely, a fool-thought.

This, however, must be said in respect to the faith of Mr. MacKay, that, while he believed in the verbal inspiration of the Bible, believed in the necessity of re-birth, believed that this re-birth was brought about by divine fiat and divine miracle, yet, it was not on these experiences he rested his hope of salvation. These concepts were all a part of his temple of knowledge and accepted by him as words of truth and verity, but not one of them secured from him the allegiance of his heart and soul and spirit to God. The concept which made him a Christian was the belief that he was the possessor of the divine favour, not because of the nature, nor the quality of the Soul of God, but because that salvation and freedom from the consequences of sin had been purchased for him, the price paid, the blood of Christ. This was the commonly accepted teaching of that time, a concept of salvation universally believed and taught by Protestant Christendom from Reformation times. "The blood of Jesus Christ, His Son, cleanseth us from all sin." "Without shedding of blood, there is no remission of sins."

This was a teaching which came down to us because the idea of it was embodied in the temple services of Jerusalem— their varied forms of animal sacrifices, which were to appease or take away the wrath of God. As the blood of these sacrificial animals made atonement for sin so the great atonement, the blood of Jesus Christ, was the great Healer of the sins of all nations. Salvation by purchase with blood and con-version by miracle, was therefore the basic faith of Mr. MacKay and his school.

The first public utterance which I was given the privilege to hear which might be deemed the beginning of the trend away from the standard of faith illustrated by Mr. MacKay's book, was a sermon preached by the late Reverend Fredrick B. Duval, D.D., in Knox Church, Winnipeg, where he was pastor, and where I worshipped during the winter months when in attendance at Manitoba College.

Seven years had passed by since I had read and believed "Grace and Truth." These seven years were momentous years in the history of the Christian Church. In this period men were studying the Bible as they had never studied it before, but this was not that they might find through it the way to the Kingdom of God. It was that they might discover errors, omissions, emendations in the text, and whatever else might go to prove that it was the workmanship of man only. Everywhere men were reading it with assiduity that they might make some new discovery which would lend its aid in discountenancing the viewpoint that it was of miraculous origin, a product of the Divine Mind.

Doctor Duval was on occasions a prince among preachers, and this morning was one of the occasions. He so far excelled his usual self that he was asked to repeat the achievement for the benefit of certain absentees amongst his membership who had heard of his great and excellent sermon. But the occasion and the sermon could not be repeated and those who were not there had to suffer the loss which their absence occasioned.

If an interested audience is a source of inspiration to a preacher, or a public speaker, Doctor Duval must have found himself encouraged by the rapt interest displayed by the whole of his large audience on that occasion. I can still see the thoughtful face of Doctor John M. King, our revered Principal, becoming increasingly thoughtful as the sermon proceeded. I recall the pleased appearance on the countenance of Reverend George Bryce, LL.D., Professor of Literature and History, as he listened to choice phrase after phrase in a most telling sermon, and relished them as sweet morsels under his tongue. Once more in vision, I observe the strained tension of the choir as if afraid to bespoil for that listening audience, by even a muscular movement of the face, the sacred sanctity of the hour and the words of the preacher. Over all that packed auditorium, a hushed stillness prevailed, for every one felt an uncanny something which told them that the preacher was handing out fresh from his inspired soul, a new light on an old doctrine. I hear once more in memory the sincere judgment of Hugh John MacDonald, the son of the noted Canadian premier, as of a man into whose soul there had come a new faith, "We have listened to a great sermon this morning."

And we had. I doubt very much if Doctor Duval ever before or after, equalled it. Certainly he never surpassed it. For myself, all the pleasure which comes from reading a book in which every sentence is a gem of literary art; all the pleasure which comes from hearing a great orator; all the pleasure which comes from seeing an edifice in which there is no architectural flaw, all this was mine as I listened to his theme:

"Except a man be born again, he cannot see the kingdom of God."

But the emphasis of Doctor Duval was not on the word "again," as was Doctor MacKay's, but on the word "see." For the word "again" he chose the alternative, "anew."

It was an inspiring occasion for that large audience, not only for the manner of telling, but also because of the subject matter. He told of the wonderful privileges and blessings enjoyed by those to whom was given the power to "see"; to those who could truly be called the "Children of Light." He told of the forgiveness and mercy awaiting everyone who would approach the mercy-seat in quest of that forgiveness and mercy. He told of the energizing power at the service of all who would honestly and truly set out to reach the kingdom. He told of the conquests over evil potential in every human soul which would strive to enter in at the strait gate. All this he told with an eloquence which could be felt but not described.

"Conversion is a necessity," he exclaimed, "not because man is born with a nature depraved, but because he must have a true concept of God—a concept of Him, as 'Our Father,' a father of love, forgiveness and mercy—every man an heir of His love; every man an heir of His forgiveness; every man an heir of His mercy; vision and an appreciation of this heritage, this is the requisite need of every man. This is conversion."

Doctor Duval would have had us believe that our concept of God, that upon this would depend our present happiness, as well as our hope for the future. Upon it would depend also the manner of life we should live upon this earth. If we had a wrong concept of the Soul of God, this would throw our whole life out of focus. If we had a right concept, then the light would become our servant, and we would see all essential things in their right relationships. We should know truth, and to know truth and follow it would make us happy, hopeful and useful members of the human family. 'We would then live our lives as we ought to live them, or as near the "ought" as our imperfect natures would permit us so to do.

Here then, was a different emphasis, and a different interpretation of the text from that of MacKay's. It was not antagonistic to the teaching of "Grace and Truth." Both men were looking at the same thing from a different viewpoint. Both of the men believed in conversion as a necessary requirement to enter into the Kingdom of Heaven. But while Mr. MacKay looked upon it as a miracle wrought through the unmerited grace of God, the other saw in it only a new mental outlook occasioned by the coming to the human mind of a new and added light and received in the usual way in which all concepts of faith are received.

Both of the men, however, side-stepped the great problem, why to one division only of the human family was given the benefits of this renewal, this enlightenment, while to all the rest, who were equally the spring of God, was this grace denied? This was the great question respecting human destiny to which a satisfactory answer had not, as yet, been given.

The Pharisee would have had his ready answer. "The reason is obvious; the superiority of our class above all others."

Such a statement, however, would not quench the desire of the sinner for a better treatment from God— "Why not be merciful to me, though a sinner?"

No, the question why some were included and the others left out was not answered, but the preacher came dangerously near it on two occasions in that morning's service. He might have as well, however, anticipated the present-day thought and declared—"All saved; none excepted"—for that was the impression which he left on that large audience of thoughtful and cultured minds gathered there from the four quarters of a great city. If God possessed these attributes of love, forgiveness and mercy, which was pictured so graphically by the preacher, and in a perfect degree, how could it be possible that some only were included as beneficiaries of these attributes and the others left out? The heart of every person in that audience answered, "This would be impossible with a God such as the Christ—concept pictured Him to be."

Our next discovery of this trend away from the old faith was the reading of a work compiled by a group of English-church clergymen. This was a commentary on this same passage of the Scriptures from which the other two men had obtained their themes, the one for his book, the other for his sermon.

Like Doctor Duval, these men called for no miracle to effect the religious experience of conversion which all agreed was a necessary requirement for membership in the Kingdom of Heaven. It called for no supernatural power to effect the change only the right use of the gifts with which man was natally endowed, these energized as the occasion required, by the spirit of God. The change was a psychological change. It was a change of attitude of mind toward God brought about by the discoveries made by the spirit of man in the realm of the spiritual.

Their viewpoint turned on their interpretation of four selections from the Scriptures, two from the Old Testament and two from the New. From the New, the two attributed to Christ, "Except a man be born again"; and, "Except a man be born of water and the spirit, he cannot enter into the kingdom of God." The two from the Old Testament, "In the beginning," the first word of the Bible, and "Let us make man in our image," were quoted to explain the significance of the two quoted from the New; deduced to support their theory of the meaning of conversion and the nature of man. Their interpretation of the meaning of the passages quoted from Saint John's Gospel was undoubtedly coloured and inspired by recent discoveries of science in the realm of nature. In the words "water" and "spirit," of the second passage, they found confirmation for the teaching which put them in agreement with the scientists and in harmony with their discovery of the law of renewal by growth. They saw in these two words an allusion on the part of Christ to what took place at the creation of the world. The "spirit" was the Spirit of God, and the "water" was the symbol of the "mist" and "chaos" the condition in which the scientists found this world when they went back for enough to discover it. Out of this "chaos and "mist" came this ordered material universe to-day where we live and move and have our being, and it was the Spirit of God brooding over it which wrought the change and created the order.

In regard to the word translated "again" in the ancient version of our Bible, they substituted for this word the one which stands as the first word of the Scriptures. The language in which the conversation between Nicodemus and Jesus took place was not the Greek, the language in which the Gospel was written, but the Aramaic. The Greek word bears among others, the translation "in the beginning." It was thus that these commentators interpreted it. As "in the beginning" the creation of the universe was effected, not instantaneously by command of God, creating something out of nothing, but by a slow and orderly process, working—constantly and continuously, changing the "chaos" and "mist" from order to higher order, and sentient beings from one form of life to higher forms, so, also, according to the allusion of Christ in the use of these two words, is the method by which the renewal of man takes place. The same spirit at work; the same method; the same goal in perspective. From standard to higher standard, and from stage to higher stage, an added something at every stage, making of life something; more worthwhile and of man something greater than he was at every preceding stage of his career, so man rises to higher and higher standards of achievement in life and character, and this true of the whole of the human family, not one excepted.

These commentators did not deny the reality of the religious experience which we call conversion. They defined it differently. With them it was a stage in the growth of the religious life of man by which he came in conscious possession of the concept that God is "Our Father" and that we are His offspring—a concept which set before man, in new perspective, the duties and responsibilities of his life and gave to him a hopeful, optimistic viewpoint of the destiny of man, not only his own destiny, but that of the whole human family as well. This is the viewpoint which has caught the ear and captured the heart of present-day Christendom and is now being rapidly substituted by enlightened Christianity in the place of the viewpoint of the old school of thought.

Under the regime of the old concept of conversion, organized Christianity became the fruitful field of hypocrisy and charlatanism—the one making pretence to the possession of a miraculous regeneration which they never experienced and to the lack of which their subsequent, selfish and loveless lives bore ample testimony – while the others devoted themselves to the unenviable vocation of creating many and unhappy divisions in the human family, a family which, in the purpose of God, was meant to constitute an affectionate, and happy and united Christian brotherhood.

THE MYSTERY INFLUENCE OF
GOD IN HUMAN LIFE

IT WAS AT THE BEGINNING of this crucial period in the history of Christian idealism that I began my Gospel ministry. All Gospel ministers of that period were called upon to walk upon waters boisterous and deep, but many of them kept discreetly off the waters and saved themselves, not from responsibility of decision, but from its worry. Whether they themselves and the people whom they served were the better for this discretion, it is not possible for others to say. Neither at Manitoba College, Winnipeg, nor at Knox, Toronto, both of which institutions I attended, for my preparatory training, was there a ripple upon the surface of the water. The discoveries of science, and its likely influence upon orthodox Christianity was viewed by both institutions with complacent indifference.

At Queen's University, Kingston, it was entirely different. Attending there to take a short course in theology and philosophy after my graduation, I was surprised, on my arrival, to find the atmosphere of the university in a state of ferment. Wherever the students foregathered, there was but one topic of conversation and discussion. On the streets as they walked together, in their classrooms after lectures; in their evening assemblies, at table together, their one subject was the effect the doctrine of evolution was having on popular beliefs concerning the destiny of man. Many a fierce battle of words was fought amongst them, radicals and conservatives, and the radical did not always come off second best.

Being a stranger, I sat and listened to these discussions, but when alone, I meditated; and as often as my thoughts turned in the direction of the movement, my memory recalled to me a familiar passage of the Scriptures, which I deemed very appropriate:

"Refrain from these men and let them alone; for if this counsel, or this work be of men, it will come to nought; but, if it be of God, ye cannot overthrow it; last haply ye be found even to fight against God."

Doubtless there is nothing covered but which the future will eventually reveal; and nothing hidden but which in due time shall be made and oftentimes it is a good policy to follow this counsel, if only the circumstances would make possible the opportunity until these desired disclosures were made; but, to me, this was quite impossible in view of the atmosphere of the University at that time.

Shortly after my arrival there, on the invitation of a friend of mine, I was at table one evening with a group of students. We were hardly seated when a young man opposite me inquired, I was going to say demanded, where I, coming from another university, stood in respect to this movement?

There remained for me no alternative other than to make some kind of an answer. If I said I side-stepped it, they would have named me a coward. If I said I side-tracked it, students are horribly cruel to one another at times, they would have said I was a fool. It might side-track me, as it did the student who was making the enquiry, but I, certainly, could not side-track it. If I said I opposed it, there would have been a battle royal on, one which would have continued past midnight if the boys could have afforded the time. But I had no occasion nor desire to do anyone of these three things.

I had not been for three years under the efficient tutorship of Principal John M. King of Manitoba College without realizing that in respect to one's own temple of truth, one's own faith, every tub must sit on its own bottom, every herring hang on its own tail. Neither had I been left without instruction as to the criteria unto which all concepts, claiming to be true, require to be found in harmony, before being accepted and made a part of our temple of Christian faith. I had no hesitation, therefore, in taking what I believed to be a proper attitude towards this movement, now occupying such a prominent place in the thoughts of the whole body of these university students.

"Do you mean," I began, "the concept concerning Gehenna?"

That was the one subject, among the many argued, around which their discussions chiefly revolved. Receiving an affirmative answer, I continued,

"Truth cannot contradict itself, Mr. MacKay." (That was the student's name.) If there is an apparent contradiction between the discoveries of science and human faith, in such a case one of them at any rate, is wrong, and both of them may be. The problem of the destiny of man is one wholly within the realm of faith. Man can believe what he likes for himself, but when he comes to call upon others to believe what he believes, he must show cause why he makes such a demand. To me, there are three questions to be answered before I can be expected to give either an affirmative or a negative answer.

"First, is the doctrine, 'All saved, none excepted,' corroborated by the teachings of Christ?

"Second, does it appear reasonable to expect that this should be the destiny of all?

"Third, Will such a faith receive corroboration from human experience?

"However," I added, "there is something about this faith concerning the destiny of man which seems to commend it, if it can be proven believable. A hope for all of the human family instead of to a division of them, and that hope based on what we believe to be a truer concept of the Soul of God, is surely a more commendable faith, comparing it with the one in which you and I were first taught to place our trust, Mr. MacKay." That was my reply to him.

Thirty and six years have passed by since this incident and this conversation occurred. What have I seen and heard all these years since concerning this movement? Has it lost prestige and power during these thirty-six years since? These new-thought school-men still teach that when man goes to his long home, there is a place prepared, a place of pleasantness, and that not for one division of the human family only, special favourites of heaven, but for every member, not one excepted. They still teach the Christ-concept, that God is "Our Father," a Father to be loved, not a Judge to be feared. They still teach that man was created in the image of God, and endowed with an energy which promises to lead him from stage to higher stage in life until he has reached the stature of a perfect man. They still teach, that Christ was crucified by wicked men because of His loyalty to this truth. But more than that, for one who affirmed these things then, there are a thousand who affirm them now; for one who had these things in consideration then, there are tens of thousands who have them in their thought and faith now. There has been progress, in the number of those who have departed from the old-time thought concerning Gehenna, a marked increase in the number of disciples who profess not to believe in it. Is this, or is it not, progress truthward?

During all these years since, I have continued a student of the movement, comparing and testing its teaching with the experiences with which I was compelled to face in my pastoral ministry. Some of these experiences I have already recorded. Others I shall now proceed to record as evidence that as far as the practical experiences of an evangelical ministry is concerned, there is not, nor can there be, any division made in the human family; but, to all, he must proclaim alike a Father who loves, forgives and shows mercy to every member of His family, not one excepted.

If there is any time more than another when a satisfying Gospel of this kind is needed, it is when one is on their death-bed, and where death has become a disturbing thought, not merely because it means the parting with friends here but because of the reception which the dying man fears he will receive on the other side from Him who inhabiteth eternity. At such a time he cannot be counselled to go back on his past life and re-live it, make amends where amendment would be required. He cannot be counselled to do better in the future. For him there is neither past nor future as far as this earthly life is concerned. Under circumstances of this kind, the minister must have a positive and a definite message which is capable of meeting the requirements and the need of the hour; something which will give the dying man strength to do battle with his fears and cast them out; something which will take away his aversion to death and give him unwavering courage to face it; something which will change his cheerless, hopeless outlook upon the future and give him instead the vision of a God whose heart of love, whose all-embracing mercy and whose unlimited forgiveness guarantees for him the eternal happiness of an eternal home.

In respect to this, we repeat, the Evangelical minister must have decided views. It is the one question, which, above all others, he cannot escape. He cannot hedge around it. He cannot run away from it. He must have some message which will solve every man's need and problem, not one excepted.

Thirty-six years of experience has taught me that the message which can do this, and it is the only one which can, is, "All saved; not one excepted"; and, the faith in this founded on Christ's concept of the Soul of God and the potentiality of man.

I was travelling along the road one day visiting my people, when I overtook an aged woman, walking along in the same direction and carrying a basket on her arm, as she returned from the village store where she had been doing some domestic purchasing.

I invited her to ride. When she was seated, she made request of me, "I wish you would come in to see my son. He is very sick, and the doctor says he will never get better."

"Is he a Christian?" I enquired, as I accepted her invitation.

"I am afraid not," was her answer.

"Then," I informed her, "I would like to see him alone when I make the call."

When I entered I was introduced to a bright-looking young man, pale and thin, the victim of tuberculosis. He was sitting in an easy chair in his bedroom, his young wife standing by his side. Our introduction over, the mother beckoned to his young wife and both left the room in accord with my previous request.

"Are you a Christian?" was my introductory question to the young man, when we both found ourselves alone in this room.

"No," was the answer, "but when I get better, I am going to join the church."

What a foundation upon which to rest one's hopes for eternity!

"Oh, but I am not asking you," I replied, "what you are going to do after you get better; or at any time; but, are you now, at the present time, believing yourself to be lost or saved?"

"I suppose I am lost," came the answer, pathetically frank.

"No, no, that cannot be," was my immediate reply. "Lost you certainly are not."

I followed up this statement setting before him, as best I could, the Christ-concept of God as "Our Father." —loving, forgiving, merciful, a father to be loved, not a Judge to be feared." This Christ-concept of God I set up in contrast to, and in rebuttal of his own thought-idea, that there would be the committal of his soul into Gehenna, in retribution, and as a penalty, for the failure of his life to measure up to the standard of righteousness required of him, if the doctrines hitherto taught him were true. Such a concept of the destiny of man could bring no peace nor hope to a dying man's heart; could open no door of hope, that the sinner would be admitted forgiven into the realm and presence of the Eternal Father. Because God was his "Father," therefore, He would forgive and show mercy to His own natural child, even although that child had fallen far short of reaching the standard of life which he ought to have lived—"this was the hope and faith which I set before him.

The placing of the Christ-concept of God before the human mind is one thing, but the turning of the soul in confidence and trust towards Him who forgives and forgets is quite another. The one is the work of a teacher, but the other is the work of the Energizer of God exercised upon the spirit-life of man supplying him with the needed complement of faith and trust in God, who because He is his Father can therefore be expected to treat him as a son.

Shortly after I departed from that home, as the young man meditated on the message which I had given him, the reality of the fatherhood of God dawned upon him. Calling his mother and his wife into the room, he threw his arms around his young wife, drawing her to him in close embrace, and exclaimed exultingly, "I am not afraid to die now; God, my Father, saves me."

Before this he was afraid to die; now that fear was departed. In its place was a spirit of peace, quietude of mind and happy hope, a confidence and assurance that the gate of heaven would be open to welcome him, this attitude and changed mind coming to him as a result of believing that the concept of God which I had set before him was the true one. On the occasion of my next visit there, I discovered a new atmosphere had taken possession of the home. "I always thought I had something to do; I did not know it was God who did the saving." This was his explanation and testimony to the world of the circumstances connected with it.

It was Sunday afternoon. The telephone rang and I was called to visit a young woman, she, too, dying from tuberculosis. She was asking for baptism. The hour was fast approaching when she must leave her earthly friends, and as she drew near to the gate of death, she began to ponder over the things which she had omitted in respect to her religious life, the performance of which might gain for her a place in the kingdom. She had not been baptized. Her family belonged to a division of the church called Disciple Baptists, and as there were none of her own ministers available, rather than be without baptism, she had sent me word that she would accept the baptism of the division of the church of which I was a minister. To visit her, it meant that I would have to give up a service of public worship, which I conducted every Sunday at that hour. Making other arrangements for my church service,

I started for that home, purposing in my mind, however, that I would not perform the ordinance of baptism, though I did not so express myself either to the girl or to her parents. When I arrived, I found a concourse of her relatives there, all of them expecting that the ordinance would be administered. When I went into the house, I asked the privilege of seeing her alone, as I had done in the former instance. I followed very closely my former method of procedure, discovering, if I could, what hope was hers, and on what ground she was basing that hope. Again, the division of the human family into "lost" and "saved" was in her mind as in the mind of the young man just mentioned. Leaving this question to correct itself, I addressed myself to the one question now uppermost in her own mind—Is there salvation for me? Accompanying this uncertainty was the fear of death, not because of the tortures which were to come to her after death, but because it was death, the giving up of her friends and home and her life on earth which she was enjoying notwithstanding the dread disease which had taken possession of her. The Christ-concept of God as her Father, was the concept which I set before her, with all the significance which was associated with that concept in respect to the question of human life and human salvation.

Again that mystery influence came into evidence. All fear of death was taken away. A comforting peace and joyful hope took possession of her spirit. She did not now ask for baptism, nor did she desire it. Possessed of the reality, the artificial found no place neither in her desire, nor wish, nor thought. Death was robbed of its sting and her future of its fears. She was fortified in her spirit for this last great event of her life by the possession of a faith, in the love, forgiveness, and mercy of her eternal Father, which came to her, as all the circumstances bore ample testimony, in answer to her need from that same Father in whom she now believed.

One more instance I will add to these two. I awoke one morning with an impulse to go to see a certain woman whom I had been invited to visit. She lived outside of the bounds of our parish, with none of her own religious denomination in her immediate neighbourhood. When I arrived there I found a large group of people gathered there, notwithstanding it was early morning. I soon discovered the reason. The mother, the woman whom I had come to see, had taken suddenly ill, and her death was at any time expected. All through the night she had been asking for a minister, but both people and physician thought this unnecessary; because delirious, this mental state precluded the need of one. Psychology and physician can explain it how they will, on my arrival the woman became quite rational and continued so all the time I was there. The people stood by in wonderment as they listened to question and answer passing between us. As before, I spoke to her of the great heart of love, the all-embracing mercy and the unlimited forgiveness of the Father of whom we were the offspring. With joyful hope she exclaimed, "Then, He'll not cast me out." It was the comforting expression of her faith. These words she was repeating as I left the home, and kept repeating at intervals, I was later told, until a sudden convulsion of the body and she was dead.

Instances similar to these followed one another at regular intervals during my thirty-six years' ministry, to me, all bearing testimony that the ministry of the love, forgiveness and mercy of God is not for a division of the human family only, but for all, not one excepted.

Step by step with God, my Father,
Step by step, he leadeth me;
Step by step, His hand upholdeth
As we walk upon life's sea.

Step by step, His hand upholdeth;
Step by step, he leadeth me;
Step by step, His love inspireth
As we walk upon life's sea.

When my fears my heart assaileth,
When the billows round me roll,
Then it is my Father speaketh
Words of peace unto my soul.

Gift of strength my Father bringeth
When temptations round me surge;
Words of warning and of promise,
Heart to cleanse and soul to purge.

AN UNBROKEN, UNDIVIDED FAMILY

NOTWITHSTANDING THE MEAGER records which have come down to us, the small fragment of what must have been the teaching of Christ on this and kindred subjects, we have nevertheless some very valuable sayings of the Master from which we can deduce what was his concept concerning very many important topics bearing on human life and human destiny. Concerning the subject, the destiny of the human family, we think we have sufficient to gauge a fairly accurate conclusion that he believed and taught the possibility of recovery from sinful life and a growth in renewal for every member of the human family which would issue in each achieving his appointed goal of destiny.

The chief passage of the Scriptures on which we base our belief that this was his concept of the human family is found in the fifteenth chapter of the Gospel of Saint Luke. Here, in one of his most popular parables, dealing with the question of salvation, we have his prophecy of the human family being destined to become an undivided and an unbroken household, one in which they dwell together in the fellowship of a love as perfect as that which recovered them, and this fellowship of love continued throughout the long aeons of an endless eternity. This is set before us, not only as God's vision of the future, but as his accomplished achievement.

The story opens out with the younger of two sons seeking to break up this unity of the family, its solidarity, its oneness in aim and life. He purposes to go out and live his own life independent of the others, believing that in this way he will achieve a greater and a happier destiny than he could, remaining as a part of the one, his father's household. He believes that he would fare not so profitably if he remained at home, sharing with the others the one responsibility and reaping equally with the others the sum total of the benefits which would come from their one united effort. It is, however, in his aim of life wherein the thought of the young man exemplifies most its folly. He will depart from the home in order that he may forego the responsibility of realizing his natal potentiality and instead devote his life exclusively to pleasure.

He had no difficulty in obtaining the opportunity and the privilege of trying out the life upon which he had set his heart. The father, generously and indulgently, permitted him the opportunity and went so far as to supply him with the resources wherewith to test out the thought and discover for himself and by his experiences the folly inherently bound up in the idea. The opportunity given him, the erring youth did not take long to put a far distance between himself and his true home. Elated with the abundance of resources placed at his disposal, but having his eyes riveted on the beginning only, the end of his career does not appear to have come once in his thoughts, at least this aspect of life did not receive that consideration from him which its importance warranted.

There is progress in folly as well as in the better aspects of life. The first stage in this young man's career was the wasting of his resources with reckless prodigality. Every five dollars spent decreased his resources to that extent, and brought him that much nearer the end of his career. As five began to be added to five in his programme of expenditure, his resources diminished accordingly, but still the young man took no note of what the end would be. Thus it is with all the experiments of folly. They are self-destructive, but carry in their wake an unexplainable blindness to the issue. Their strength perishes with the use made of them, yet the victim takes no stock of his diminishing resources, and when ended, his utter lack of means to replenish the supply.

The ways of folly lead but to one end. Inherent in them are those qualities which defeat their own end and purpose, which destroy but do not build up. From stage to stage, from lower to still lower, from less to still less, the progress of the young man was onward, but it was downward, not upward. We say a wilful waste is a woeful want. It was so in this case. Diminishing resources and diminishing strength soon brought him to the end of that way of life. The fool-thought promised him a life of pleasure, but instead; supplied him with an apple goodly in outward appearance, but rotten at the core.

Circumstance determines the occasion, which in turn, determines the choices of our life. The day on which his resources ran out was the day when, unfortunately for his fool-thought, nature for some unaccountable reason went out on a holiday and failed because of this to make provision for the usual harvest. The blight of famine came upon the land. The young man had made no provision for the uncertainties of life. Herein was folly number two. There are uncertainties in life, and wisdom demands that we be alert to discover them, their likelihood, their whereabouts, and the time when they will likely make their appearance. Wisdom requires that we anticipate and make provision for all these probable emergencies when we can.

Nature, however, is a very kind mother to us. Notwithstanding the element of uncertainty inherent in herself, she makes friendly overtures to us, and comes readily to the assistance of anyone desiring to meet the emergencies resulting from her own uncertainties This young man might make complaint that Fate was very unkind to him in that it brought these two circumstances together—the end of his resources and the famine in the land—at one and the same time. In his case, however, it was the very opposite. The universe, in doing this, was performing for him a very kindly act in that it was going to show to him the folly which was bound up in his fool-thought, and which had brought him to the predicament in which he now finds himself. It happened as an occurrence meant to save him from the consequences following inevitably from the life which he had chosen.

The possibility of these two things happening together but added emphasis to the folly of his original fool-thought. If a man will choose a fool-thought for his guide in life, he cannot expect anything other than that he will reap according to his choice. If the land was groaning with plenty when his resources ran out, his friends would have helped him freely and unhesitatingly from their plenty. Their failure to do so revealed to him folly number three in his wrong concept of life; revealed that the friendship of those whom he had taken into his life as a substitute for a father's love and a brother's companionship could not stand the test which his changed circumstances in life required of them. They were friends who had been attracted to him for what they could get out of him; who had joined themselves to him for the sake of obtaining a share of the profits and pleasures which his prodigal and spendthrift habits had made possible. The end of his resources taking away the likelihood of any further benefits, caused them to make a quick withdrawal of further companionship with him, disclosing to him the true nature of their pretended friendship.

It is always so with the friendships of folly. They are out to bleed their friends, and when they cannot bleed them any more, they forsake them. His were tried. They proved that his faith in them had been misplaced; that he had been made the victim of their hypocrisy and charlatanism; and, that if he was to profit from what service others could render him, he would have to seek an entirely different quality in the friendship of the persons whom he should hereafter make his companions in life.

Left wholly to himself, he came to himself. He discovered that his former concept of life was an entirely erroneous one. In every test made of it, the inherent folly and falsity of it was disclosed. A fool-thought it was; that, and nothing more. He discovered also, that the sonship to which his father had a right and a claim, had been denied that father, and that this sin against his father had brought him no prosperity, as he thought it would, but the very opposite.

As he meditated, not having acted the part of a son, he could not now claim the relationship of a son. Yet, to be in his father's household, even as a hired servant, would be, he concluded, better than to be outside of that household. He would, therefore, he resolved, go back to his home and to his father. Herein was a faith-concept founded on a sure foundation, and therefore a concept of wisdom and truth. The fool-thought had brought to him an hilarious hour followed by an eternal want. The faith-concept brought him back to his father's home and in security and safety; brought him back to a father's love and to a father's protection and eternal care.

On his arrival back at the home from which he should never have deserted, there came to him the rediscovery of an old truth—that though he had ceased to be a son, the father had not ceased to be a father; that his return to that home was made dependent not upon his own claims, or rights, or resolutions, but upon the reality of his father's love. The fatherhood of his father, opened the door, threw his arms around him in enthusiastic welcome, and restored him, not to the place of a servant, but to the only place which would guarantee the unity of the family and make of it an undivided, an unbroken household.

But the story of the lesson of the parable is not yet ended. There is another half to it. There was another son, he, too, in his spirit—life, an enemy to the unity, the solidarity, the oneness of the family home; he, too, having the spirit, which if allowed to express itself, would bring about a division followed by a tragical ending of a united home life. He had maintained himself up to this hour a devoted and loyal son. In the spirit of filial love, he had succeeded where the other brother had failed. Now, however, as a brother, he discovers himself to be an ignominious failure. In this spirit, there was in the elder brother, a deplorable want. The one son was an enemy to the spirit of the home, lacking the spirit of sonship; the other its enemy by his want of the spirit of brotherhood.

The failure of the two brothers to maintain the unity of the family was due to their failure to realize their potentiality; to make even a partial effort to achieve it. Of all potentialities gifted to man, the power to love is the greatest, the noblest, the best. In respect to this potentiality, this power, Jesus has issued his challenge to the world, "Be ye perfect, even as your heavenly Father is perfect."

In respect to this challenge, the beloved Apostle, John, has added his comment, informing us that the Heavenly Father is moved by a Divine restlessness, a Divine dissatisfaction, from which His spirit cannot have release until every member of the human family has answered the challenge, realizing each one his own potentiality, not one excepted.

Thus is the Goal set by the Divine Mind for achievement by the human race, the Goal also set by the Divine Mind for Himself, and we cannot conceive, since He has made no provision for it, that there can be with Him any miscarriage or failure in its achievement.

Believe me, if all those dear mercies of God,
Which we cherish so fondly to-day,
Were to fade from our faith
Like summer months passing away;
Thou wouldst still make us know,
As this moment Thou doth,
That the safety of man is Thy will;
And around every ruin of sin-ravished lives,
Mercies of grace surroundeth them still.

It is not while virtue and strength are our own,
And our life without cloud or a fear,
That the words of our Christ
Mean so much to our life,
And God's salvation needed so near;
For the man whom God loves He will never forsake,
But He sure will love on to the close;
And the world which Christ loved
On the cross when he died,
That same world he still loves since he rose.

MILLIONS OF CHRISTIANS IN AMERICA DESERTING THEIR CHURCHES

O VER AGAINST THIS steady progress in Christian thinking which we have chronicled as having taken place during the last fifty years in the history of Christianity, we have to consider the steady depletion which has been taking place at the same time in the various branches of the Christian churches in respect to their membership and church attendance, a drifting away which is not ending, but rather increasing in momentum as the years pass by. The attention of Protestantism in the United States is being called to this feature of the Church's life by *The American*, a high-class magazine published in New York. In a carefully-prepared article by William Corbin, in its August number, 1937, he outlines a survey of conditions which he has discovered in his own country under the title, "Why I Don't Go to Church."

In this article he informs us that he was brought up in childhood to attend a Protestant Sunday School and that of his own desire and accord he attended church in young manhood until he was past twenty years of age. Then he drifted away from the Church, and that without being able to give any definite reason why he did so. Drawing attention to the fact, that of the fifty million Protestants of the population of the United States, thousands of them, though religious men, are drifting away in steady stream from the Church, no longer attend its services, live as though it did not exist, he issues a challenge to the Church to show cause why he and the millions who have ceased to attend her services should not have done so.

He tells us that, as a hobby, he began to make a survey to discover, if he could, why these thousands had deserted their churches. Interviewing first those who had drifted away, he epitomized their varied answers in one telling phrase—"The Church does not give us what we want."

He followed this up by visiting different churches covering the national field, representing all the different classes of churches of Protestant Christianity within the borders of his nation from north to south and from east to west, to hear what message they had for the people. He came back, having heard no sermon, he tells us, with instructive content—nothing vital, gripping, or enlightening said—nothing to inspire— nothing enriching personality, stimulating action, and ennobling thought and motive— nothing only, "ancient history and dry rot . . ."

He then went to the clergy with a pertinent question, a definite query—"What has the Church to offer that is unique, peculiar to it, that is not to be found in better form elsewhere?" He came back without an answer.

Finally, he turned to two bodies of divinity students, the graduating classes of Union Theological Seminary in New York and the Yale Divinity School. From the first he "developed one of the most confusing experiences of his life," but no solution to the problem which this drift away from the Church had created.

From the second, there was less confusion and a more practical approach to the discussion, finally ending by one of the students offering an answer to the question.

"The one unique and unchanging thing which the Church has to offer, now and for ever, is the rock upon which it is built, Jesus Christ. It is Jesus Christ who is peculiar to us and unique to the world. The Church offers to you Jesus and He is offered nowhere else to-day. The Church offers you God as He is manifested through Jesus. You receive Jesus into your life. You repent; you are forgiven. You see light that you have never seen before. He becomes a living factor in your life. We teach adoration of Jesus."

To the rejoinder of Mr. Corbin, "You mean that you preachers of to-morrow are going back to the old-time religion—to basic Christianity?" there came back a unanimous answer in the affirmative.

With this answer Mr. Corbin brings his survey to an end, informing us as his closing comment upon it,

"This is what I have found so far—a feeling that the Church in order to live and function must return to primitive Christianity, the unadorned teaching of Jesus. Perhaps that is the answer. Perhaps that's what people want in church—pure religion of the old, old kind. But it isn't for me. It happened too long ago. Its background is not my background nor that of the people I know to-day. A return to unanswerable and unrationalized faith is to me a retreat from the front of action, an evasion of the needs of millions like me.

"I feel like a musician without an instrument, a student without books, a man in a strange land without guide or interpreter. Meanwhile, I, a religious man, if not a churchgoing one, continue to grope. I WISH I KNEW WHAT I SOUGHT."

This is the picture of conditions as they exist in the country south of us, set forth by a man who is in sympathy with the aims of the Church, who was once a part of it, but not now, who knows that he is living a life below the level of the achievement possible to him. Carrying in his heart the feeling of a great want, he looks to the Church to meet the needs of his life, but looks in vain. Representing the millions, who, like himself, were once attached to the Church but not so any longer, he tells us that these are to-day without a Church because the Church of to-day does not meet their needs. They are no longer Christian actors in the great drama of human life; religious, but not Christian. Who is to blame?

"The Church is at fault," is the conclusion to which he comes.

In Canada, we have a similar situation. Our Church here is as their Church there. It is not meeting the situation facing it any more than is the Church of the United States meeting theirs. The Church in the one country is an exact counterpart of the Church in the other. If there is any difference it is that the situation in our country is more aggravated. Our country is more sparsely populated, and therefore as a consequence, the going out of one member or one family means a greater loss to our Church than it does to theirs.

The little brown church in the vale, associated with the sweet memories of our childhood years, has ceased to be. It no longer makes its appeal to the people. Where I sit I look out through the window and see an agricultural area covering half a circle with a radius of sixty miles. Inside of this area there are nine Protestant churches of one denomination and about an equal number of the others. They are all putting up a tragic struggle for existence. To-day they would be closed but that their budgets are being balanced by donations from wealthy citizens and churches from distant places and cities, who have no interest in them save that they belong to their denomination, They are serving no purpose, save to provide a meeting-place for a few old people who gather there when the weather is propitious, persons who would feel that they had not properly lived out their week if they had not begun it with an hour's attendance on the Sunday meeting of these established places of worship. One of these is probably putting forth a heroic struggle to maintain a Sunday School, attended spasmodically by the children of a few of the adjacent families. Will these places of worship survive? As long as these few people survive, but no longer. The to-morrow of their expectations is a closed door, a deserted church. As to the American thousands, so to our hundreds, the Sunday-go-to-meeting-place of rural life has come to an end.

For this disheartening outlook on the to-morrow of her life, the Church herself is at fault, is the judgment of Mr. Corbin. While some of the blame because of the non-attendance of its members upon her services is to be attributed to the Church itself, it would be too sweeping a conclusion to say that the sole cause for the desertion of so many from her ranks is wholly her own fault. Those making observation of the trend of the times will have no difficulty in coming to a revised judgment from that. The Church is facing a grave situation, without doubt, but it is not so much her fault that this situation has been created as her fate. She has been made the victim of the trend of the times,

This is a peculiar age in which we live. It has something which we cannot describe but which makes it to be an age unique, possessing something not to be found in any preceding age, and will not be found in any subsequent one except in history. We have to live in this age. To get the most out of it, we will have to adapt ourselves to the conditions which this age has created for us. We must be a living people in this living, moving age. The Church, apparently, was not flexible enough to meet these changing conditions so as to hold her own successfully in the race for the capture of the changing interests of her people. This was not so much her fault, as observed, as her misfortune. She has now to pay the price in the desertion of this numerous host from her ranks. Having lost out in the first heat, will she continue so? If so, then this will be a fault and a failure, a sin from which no multitude of excuses will be able to purchase for her absolution.

The remedy is—keeping in step with progress in Christian thinking. When we say that the Church has failed, let us not forget that the Church is as its membership; is as the sum of the potentialities of its membership. Where there are no members, there is no Church. If a man leaves off attendance upon a Church's services, he must have reason for doing so. The only reason which could be counted a valid one is, that the Church did not give him the opportunity to use the potentialities with which his Maker has endowed him in such a way that the cause of Christian truth or the advance of the Christian brotherhood would be furthered by his efforts and undertakings. The Church should give opportunity and helpful service for the realization of every man's potentiality in respect to Christian effort and achievement. If it does not do this, then, that member surely has the right to withdraw from associations from which he derives no benefits.

When Mr. Corbin says that the Church is at fault, we presume he means the leaders of the Church. In his survey, it was to the leaders he went except in respect to his fellow-deserters. He went to these to discover why each one of them individually withdrew; to determine, if there was a comradeship of interests which was not being met by attendance upon the Church's services, then, discovering a common reason, discover thereby also the remedy.

To lay the blame on the clergy in the aggregate is rather an unfair procedure. There are as many grades of clergymen as there are clergymen—from the one whose preaching would do violence to the understanding of a twelve-year-old public school pupil, the teacher who has not yet himself been taught, the leader ungifted by nature with any qualifications for leadership, onward and upward from these until you come to the Fosdicks, the Jenkinses, the Gilkeys of American fame, Whose brilliance and gifts never fail to command an audience—a motley aggregation. From amongst their number you would be able to find examples for every kind of fault of which the human family is heir. On the other hand, however, also, you would be able to discover men of consecration and devotion, who would rival the best which the Church could produce in the palmiest days of her history. To single out from this mixed aggregation the ones who should be held responsible for the lost interest in the Church, resulting in the withdrawal of so many from her ranks, would be as unprofitable a task as it is impossible of performance. We choose the better part when we confine ourselves to the double task which Christianity has set for us.

The function of the Church is a twofold one. It is hers, first, to answer the question, What is Christian truth; and, next, to create a ministry of love. The truths which are associated with the name of Christ, it is hers to hasten the clay when they shall be a part of the universal knowledge of mankind. The brotherhood which he set before us as the destined goal for the human family to reach, it is hers to add to its numbers until it has become the world-wide organic unity which he prophesied it would become, embracing every member of the human family, not one left out. If the Church fails in pushing forward the establishment of the brotherhood to a nearer completion, if there has been given no impetus leading to a growth onward and upward in the lives of the people in accord with this conception of Christ of what human society ought to be, and of what one day it will be, then there has been no advance of Christianity.

Shall we say that the withdrawal of these millions from the fellowship of the Church is their withdrawal from taking any part in the creation of this brotherhood? If so, this would mean that a great tragedy is now being staged in the great drama of human life. If the idea and spirit of the Christian brotherhood, and its establishment is confined to the Church, no other agencies disseminating the idea and spirit of it, no other agencies helping to bring about the establishment of it, then it would be true that none outside of the Church could receive the benefits of Christianity and its progress would be measured by the growth in numbers of the membership of the Church. This claim doubtless some churchmen would make for the Church, some going even so far as to assert that to their own particular denomination has been given the task of establishing this brotherhood. Observation, however, proves to us that there are other agencies doing this work as well, better even than some churches are doing it.

Writing for these millions who have withdrawn from the Church in the United States, "What has the Church to offer," asks Mr. Corbin, "that is unique, peculiar to it, and that is not to be found in a better form elsewhere?" The question, put in that form, cannot receive answer. The Church has not such a possession, nor could have and continue to be a Christian Church. Denominational Christianity may profess to have such a possession; organized Christianity may also; Christian Christianity cannot. This is the claim which charlatans, quacks and racketeers put up in order to carry on their trade, but it is a claim devoid of truth. The moment that a Christian

Church piques itself on having such a possession, the spirit of the Pharisee has come in and the poor sinner is forgotten or remembered only to be despised because of his inferiority. The monopoly which can he possessed by a man of greed, and with which he goes out to exploit or crush his less privileged and more unfortunate brother, this is a monopoly impossible in the field of Christian possessions.

In the realm of religion, there should be no divided loyalties. Unfortunately there are. There is a loyalty to the denomination; and there is a loyalty to the organization. These contend for a premier place in the devotion of the people, and oftentimes in the long run the loyalty to denomination and concern in respect to the organization which win out. In this way the Christianity, which ought to occupy the first place in their loyalty and devotion, becomes crowded out, or forced to take a minor place in their interests. The denomination ought to have something higher than the denomination as its chief interest; and the organization is serving no purpose unless it is furthering the cause of Christianity.

The ideas and ideals taught by Christ are for all men, not for a section of the people. To the heritage of Christianity, the world, and not any nation or section of the people, are its heirs. The brotherhood which He came to establish is a world-wide brotherhood. "Go in and possess the land," was a command to every family and member of the tribe of Israel. Not one, old or young, was to be left behind. The possession was for the whole, not a portion of the camp. The heritage to which we give the name of Christianity is a common heritage, and no person, clique, nor clan, may claim a monopoly on any part of it.

Truth and love we must have in this life in order to live. Human experience teaches us that we can have both. "Take away the churches," said one clergyman, "and where are you at? What have you left?"

In answer, we would say that we would have left, God; and, in Canada here, ten millions of human beings with potentialities to know and love Him with all their heart and soul and mind and their neighbour as themselves. Having these, what more do we need? No, the Church need not pique itself upon being the one and only agency doing the work of God in the world, making men conscious of their partner in life. God has not left the disclosure of himself to the arts of the magicians, nor to the drum-beatings of the racketeer. The Church, if it is true to its calling, may tell us where God is to be found, and how He is to be found, but it cannot disclose Him to us. This disclosure is made through our potentialities and their realization; a realization which is made possible by the circumstances of our life and in the performance of our daily tasks. No one else can find God for us. These circumstances and tasks will be made the occasions through which we become conscious of Him. But when He is disclosed to us, we shall hear His voice, clear and distinct, and from it there can be no evasion nor departure: "Thou shalt love the Lord thy God with all thy heart, and with all thy soul, and with all thy mind"; and, "Thou shalt love thy neighbour as thyself."

Although we believe with Mr. Corbin that there are other agencies doing the same work as the Church, teaching the truths revealed by Christ concerning man and his destiny, and that these agencies are also taking an active part in the establishing of the Christian brotherhood, yet we dare not say that in the withdrawal of these millions from fellowship with the Church, they have done wisely and well. The fault may not be in the Church, but in themselves accounting for the lack of community of interests between them. Nor are we sure that these other agencies will make up for the loss which they will sustain by their refusal to associate themselves with the work of an institution Whose function is to train men to act well their God-appointed part in the great drama of human life.

In respect to these other agencies, of which schools, books and high-class magazines, stand out prominently amongst them, in so far as they are interested in Christianity and propagate the ideas and ideals of Christianity, they are the Church's helpmeets, not her rivals. It is our proud boast that Christianity cannot fail because that it has now become so woven into our best literature as to be an inseparable part of it. Truth and love have travelled so far from being possessions unique to the Christian Church that their appeal to the human mind and heart and reason will arise from so many sources as to make escape from their influence impossible for anyone of those millions who have eliminated themselves from their former weekly routine of attendance upon their Church's regular services. If these other agencies can rival the rostrums of the Church in their efficiency in doing this, so much the better for Christianity. After all it is the destiny of Christianity which comprises the Church's premier interest rather than her own.

There is a limit as to the service which these agencies outside of the Church can render us, as there is a limit also to the services which the Church can render. Both may proclaim the need. They may disclose for us the way in which this need may be met. They may call attention to the errors and weaknesses of humanity. They cannot, however, enter into our lives and transform these lives. The spirit of man in fellowship with the spirit of man, and both of these in fellowship with the Supernatural is the only way in which we may properly live out our lives upon this earth. If the Church cannot inspire that spirit, cannot arouse it and move it to express itself, if it cannot show avenues of need calling for the expression of it, then it has lost, or is losing, the opportunity for service which it ought to be rendering. From his conference with "the two bodies of divinity students whom he interviewed, "I got this idea pretty clearly," Mr. Corbin informs us; "these young ministers of 1938 agree that the Protestant Church as a sociological institution has failed."

If a failure in this aspect of its service, then in what line of endeavour can it expect to make a success? If the supreme function of the Church is to create a Christian brotherhood, which will go on adding to its membership until every member of the human family has become a part of it, not one left out, how can it become this without being sociological in its aim, in its effort, and in its achievements? The Christian Church is a sociological institution, and must be, but it is not sociological as the dance hall is sociological. It is not sociological as the theatre, the opera, the cinema show, and the circus are sociological. It is not sociological as the Kiwanis, Rotary and Freemason clubs are sociological. Not as any of these; but it is sociological as the home is sociological. Let it cease to have the unity, the spiritual fellowship of the home, and it ceases to be a Church, at least a Christian one. It has no function. It has no service to render. It has no claim nor right of attention from any member of the human family. The Church is as the home, or, it is nothing.

The home is, first of all, God-created. I know that Doctor Blacker of New York would deny this.* When he discovered man in a cellular state, "Aha," he exclaimed as he threw his hat in the air, "we have got rid of God. No person will believe now that the Supernatural has had anything to do with the origin of man."

Without eyes, there is no seeing; without ears, there is no hearing; without the consciousness of God, there is no and man sinks to the status of the beasts in the field; without the confirmations of faith, there is no faith. Having eyes and ears and the power to know and believe in God, I cannot conceive of one hundred graduates of Toronto University, not divinity students, but physical scientists far down in their laboratory, seeing that cell, that atom, that speck of dust, too small to be seen with the naked eye, seeing that embryonic man in potentiality, seeing there in the to-morrow of that atom's life, a Wilberforce, a Lincoln, an Opie, a Longfellow, an Aristotle, a Napoleon, a Luther, a Calvin, seeing all this and no worshipful spirit. I cannot conceive it. But I could conceive of them all on their knees, and with tear-filled eyes because of the deep emotion of their hearts, exclaiming in unison, "How noble is man! How great is God!"

To get rid of the consciousness of God, to get rid of faith and knowledge in respect to Him, is not proof of His non-existence. But it is proof of the lopsided development of too many units of the human family. The greatest thing about man is his potentiality, the unity of potentialities which we entitle his personality. The greatest of his potentialities is his power to love. The source of this potentiality is God, but it cannot be realized except on the basis of a companionship between complementary associates united as one on the basis of love. Herein is our premier interest in life, and there is nothing in our life nor in the possibilities of our life which should be allowed to take a premier place to this, as there is nothing in factual life that is superior to it.

There is born in the city of London, England, a new unit of the human family. To it has been given the potentiality of fatherhood. There is born another unit in the city of New York, USA. To it has been given the potentiality of motherhood. These two potentialities are associate and complementary. The one potentiality cannot be realized except by realizing the potentiality of the other. Yet, the Atlantic Ocean divides them.

The one grows up, sees many maidens, admires them, enjoys their company, but nothing more. The other likewise grows up in her city; meets many young men, admires them, enjoys their company; that, and nothing more. Circumstance brings the young man to New York. (Circumstance is but another name for the Supernatural. Uncontrolled, unguided circumstance is non-existent.) He meets this young American woman. Immediately, or after a period of acquaintanceship, there comes into the experience of both of them that bond of union, call it mystic or mysterious, if you must have something mystic or mysterious in life, but there it is, something to which we give the name, LOVE. The source of it is not nature. Chemistry has not created it. Without it there can be no home. The complementary potentialities of two members of the human family, associated in love, has created that home.

So in respect to Christianity. So in respect to churches. The Church is a brotherhood founded on love, or it is nothing. The ministry of the rostrum may not meet the present-day need, nor provide the associations essential to the creation of the brotherhood. If not, some other way must be found. If the mountain will not come to Mahomet; Mahomet must go to the mountain. If these millions of the population of the United States and Canada, will not go where there is a ministry of love, then love must go where these millions live and move and have their being and do their daily work. It cannot be, it ought not to be, and it need not be, that any member of the human family should live out his three-score years and ten upon this earth and fail to discover anywhere his complementary associates and miss the enriching, inspiring, ennobling stimulant, which the realizing of his potentiality to love these will give him. We can do without the rostrum, but we cannot do without the ministry of love.

Nothing less than a Christian brotherhood can serve the needs of the world. There are not wanting evidences that the present-day church, in some quarters, is falling away from its first love, making courtship with fascism, communism, socialism and other organizations having to do with the solving of the problem, What shall we eat, what shall we drink, and wherewithal shall we be clothed? with the aim, of course, to have this problem solved with the least possible labour and the greatest possible returns. Caesar is quite able to look after his own dominions. But the spirit-life of man must have fellowship with his complementary associates, and this, the realm of the supernatural, is where the Church will find its liberty, its life and its love.

See Century Magazine, April, 1932

TO-MORROW

BACK TO PRIMITIVE Christianity?" This is the aim which the graduating class of Yale Divinity School, the preachers of 1938, have set for themselves to guide them in their work as leaders in the Christian Church of to-morrow, In accord with the testimony of *The American*, a high-class magazine of New York, publishing the survey conducted by their contributor, William Corbin, referred to in our preceding chapter. This is the preaching which will stop the drift away from the Church which has been going on for the last fifteen years and which is increasing in momentum as the years roll along.

The cry, "Back to Christ," was a very popular one a few years ago, but now fast waning in its popularity. The suggestion is worthless. "It isn't for me," Mr. Corbin informs us, and in this he says he is voicing the mind of all the millions, who, like himself, were once members of the Protestant Church in the United States, but are so no longer. Whatever these millions need, which will restore them to the Church, that need certainly will not be met by the production of a meaningless imitation of a departed past, even if it were possible to produce the imitation. The reproduction of the past is certainly impossible to man, and it does not appear anywhere in evidence as included in the plan and purpose of God.

The great Teacher of Nazareth lived his thirty years of fruitful life and then departed as all men must. What contribution did he make to the world's thought and the world's religion? Much, very much indeed, and of so high a quality that we see in his teachings, when fully understood and followed, the achievement of the destiny of the human family as well as the destiny of each member of the family. In the two thousand years which have passed since, there have been added additions, emendations, and barnacle encrustments which are sapping the very life out of these teachings. If by "back 'to Christ" is meant the removal of these so as to set before us his teachings in their truthful simplicity, then this is an undertaking profitable and which will add to the sum total of the agencies which will push forward the aim and purpose of God to a more perfect completion. To single out the principles of right conduct, universal in their application and eternal in their endurance, which comprised the content of much of his teaching; to discover those ideas which have come down to us from the far-distant past, and to which he gave enlightenment, wider application, and a new emphasis; to do this, would be to do a service which could issue but in one result, the advancement of the kingdom of God and the betterment of the manhood comprising that kingdom.

This does not seem, however, to be the meaning attached to the phrase, either by Mr. Corbin or the embryonic preachers of 1938 whom he interviewed. Judged by the answer which he records as having been received from one of the students, and to which all the others gave their unanimous assent, the idea embodied in this phrase would appear to be a magical, mysterious use of the personality of Christ, and this personality in some magical, mysterious way, made to become a substitute for our natal and God-created personality.

"We offer you Jesus."

"You receive Jesus."

"Christ re-created in you."

Meaningless phrases all of them, without reality or possibility of achievement!

The Church has been too long under the cloven hoof of magic and mysticism. We want something more practical to meet the needs of this present age. Even the Holy Grail, that symbol of the fellowship of social comradeship and friendship, so beautiful in its simplicity, could not escape, but had to be metamorphosed by these mystic men into a magician's wand. If it is to be a choice between commonsense and nonsense, let us by all means keep away from the latter. Why not take Christ at his own estimate of himself? If not, then the estimate of his immediate followers? Should we do so, we shall not find anything in the judgment of these which will support the teachings of the magician, the charlatan, the quack and the racketeer. We shall find instead, the beauty and the power of the simple and unadorned truths with which his name is associated.

The Christian religion is not a plant native to the soil of this country. Its native home is Palestine. The religious system into which we were born and of which we have become a part, came to us originally from the Jewish people. We have adopted their faith and their system. We have entered into the heritage which was once exclusively theirs. We have adopted their view-point of the supernatural; their synagogue worship; their weekly cessation from secular labour; all this, but much more. We have adopted it, however, only because that system suffered changes at the hands of Christ, one of their own people, which placed their system at the disposal of other nations of the world, a departure from the old which made it possible that it could be adopted by nations and peoples other than the Jewish.

The greatest change made in this system was in respect to their concept of God. The background of their whole system was the concept of God as a God of 'wrath." Our religious system has adopted the Christ-concept of God as a God of "love." The whole of the teachings of Jesus was founded on this more enlightened and more rational concept. On what authority did he presume to make this change?

To his contemporaries, it was because he was "a teacher sent from God." This was the view held by that scholarly

Pharisee, Nicodemus, and to this belief he continued to adhere right up to the end. The God of Nicodemus, was the God of the Jewish faith. He was a God over all, but also, Immanuel, God-with-us. Jesus was sent by this God, according to his faith, to the Jewish people, to discover to them what the mind of this God was concerning the Jewish nation. It was not good news to him to be told that his nation was not a favourite of heaven that theirs was not a superior nation, that if there was any benefit to come to them, it could only be by coming to other nations as well. There was to be, Christ informed this Jew, a co-partnership among the nations of the world to build up an organization which would embrace all the nations of the world, but these would be united together to form this new organization, not on the basis of mutual agreements, but upon the basis of love.

This was not pleasing to this Jew, because he did not like the thought that his nation should be reduced to the status of equality with the other nations of the world. He desired to hear how his nation was going to mount to the top over all others, and hold these others in subjection under their heel, as they were being held then under the heel of other nations.

The answer of Jesus was, "You do not like this for your own nation, why then should you wish to impose on other nations that which is not agreeable nor profitable to your own?"

But how could love become a bond of union among nations? Nicodemus could understand how it could become a bond of union between the sexes. He could understand how it could become a bond of union between different members of the home. He could even see how it could become a bond of union between different members of the clan, the tribe all of one blood. How could one nation come to love another nation? How could such things be? This was something away beyond his comprehension. Yet this, Jesus taught, was to be the to-morrow of this world's life.

Nicodemus accepted this idea of the destiny of his nation and of mankind, but only after he had accepted the idea of Christ as "a teacher sent from God." This was essential. Without this faith, he would have been as the great majority of his people were, unable to accept the teachings of Jeans concerning his nation.

We have on record another estimate of Christ, given by one of his closest followers. In accord with his followers, he was a man unto whom the spirit of the Supernatural had been given "in no sparing measure."* He was a man above men, because he was in the mind of this loyal disciple endowed with a potentiality far above the average, a potentiality greater than that of any of the teachers who had preceded him, or any, we could add, who have since followed him. But a great potentiality requires a great energy to achieve its realization. So, in addition to his potentiality, he was gifted with this energy, but as the need arose. This was Christ in the viewpoint of his contemporaries in sympathetic loyalty to him; the viewpoint of the Christ who set before the world the idea of a world-wide brotherhood founded on love, and taught his disciples to seek its realization.

The judgment of these two, the years since have substantially confirmed. To his wisdom and faith we owe the religious system which to-day bears his name. It is the Jewish system of religion brought up to date. Unique and great in respect to his wisdom, his potentiality, and his spirit, he comes before us not as our God, but as our elder brother, our teacher and our exemplar. Was he in possession of a spirit-life, an emanation from God, his Father? So is also every member of the human family. Was he conscious of the Supernatural as a daily partner in his daily life? So may every person be who will exercise sense and reason in respect to the daily occurrences of his daily life. Was he capable of a love, forgiving, merciful, a spirit akin to that of his Father in heaven, and on the basis of which he was establishing his world-wide brotherhood? His prayer as he was being nailed to the cross—Father forgive them for they know not what they do—-is the answer and the example for all mankind to follow. Had he the courage of his convictions and a loyalty to truth which he would support even unto death? So ought all people to have, if the need arose for a similar loyalty.

Though unique, he bases his appeal for a world-wide brotherhood on the possessions which he and all men hold in common, and because a common possession, they are therefore capable of being knitted together into an organic unity, enjoying the comradeship and fellowship of a common love. We revere Christ. We adore him. This, not because of his mystic personality, but because of the ideas and ideals which he released and handed down to us, an inheritance unto which all men, without exception, have become heirs. We revere and adore him also because of the institution of the brotherhood which he established and which also bears his name and which we have still with us, an institution so magnificent and noble and perfect in its conception that there is nothing left for us to do now except to carry it on to its completed realization.

Our personality is not a commodity which we can give away nor exchange for another. It is the sum of all our potentialities. In respect to our nature-life, we have been endowed with powers to see, to hear, to feel. In respect to our intelligence, we have been endowed with powers to think, to reason, to remember, to plan, to purpose, to will. In respect to our spirit-life, we have been endowed with powers to believe, to hope and to love. Now none of these powers, whether of nature-life, intelligence, or spirit-life, stand unrelated to each other, but all are knitted together as co-workers to form that organic unity which we call our person, or our personality. I am that person which these endowments have made me. Another has the same kind of endowments, but by reason of a difference in degree of these potentialities, the person is different. So Christ, He had all these which we have, and we have all that he had. We cannot barter away any of these potentialities. They are our life. Some of them we can destroy; others we cannot. But the substitution of one personality for another is a thought as absurd as it is impossible of achievement.

In addition to all this, we have the power to plan, to purpose, to will to make these potentialities serve our thoughts and our desires. We can choose and we do choose, which of two courses we shall follow. Here again marks a difference between persons, in the difference in their desires and in the difference which they will make of their potentialities. In this aspect of our life, we can receive and we do receive helpful service from our fellow man—in the correction of desire, the training of thought and the development of potentiality, purpose and will.

The foremost service rendered to us by Christ is in respect to our spirit-life. There is an interest which abideth forever; an interest which man cannot escape; an interest which is superior to all other interests of life; an interest from which man cannot be disassociated because it is a part of himself. The one word which sums up that interest is the word, "supernatural." Man cannot run away from the supernatural because it is a part of him, and he is a part of the supernatural.

Man is the product of life. The mountain is the product of law, of the forces of nature. The electric bulb is the product of both. In the latter we see an achievement of human life taking the forces of nature and utilizing them so that man is able to live out his life to better advantage than he could without these creations of his intelligence. It is supreme wisdom on the part of man to discover in order that he may utilize the laws appertaining to nature. It is a still higher and nobler wisdom to seek out and discover the laws appertaining to the supernatural world. It is the belief of Doctor Henry Drummond that when we have discovered the one, we have discovered the other. Be that as it may, one thing is certain, they cannot be, and they will not be, antagonistic and contradictory, the one to the other.

Man is the product of life; so are the beasts of the field. To live their lives, both of them need more than nature and its laws. They need the Supernatural, and, according to that need, the Supernatural is a co-partner with both in their lives. But herein lies the difference. Man is conscious of God as his partner in life. The beasts of the field are not. Man knows the partner with whom he lives and moves and has his being, and without whose partnership and aid he could not live. He feels the touch of the Hand that feeds him. He hears the voice of the Leader who guides him. He sees His works spread out in plenteous supply all around him. In the circumstance favourable, and the circumstance unfavourable, his heart says, There is God. This consciousness it is which satisfies his mind, energizes his will and gives peace to his heart. It is in the measure in which he possesses this consciousness he will be able to love God.

This being so, the premier truth which we should seek to discover, comprehend and believe is, that the supernatural is in partnership with the natural, that God is in partnership with man. To the man who is not conscious of this partnership, to this man there is no God. He is as the beasts of the field. In consciousness of the union of the natural and the supernatural, of the nature-life and the spirit-life, the consciousness of the energizing influence which is going on in our lives, the consciousness of Immanuel, God-with-us, man views the possibilities of greatness with which his potentiality is endued. Herein, he knows, lieth his strength. Other interests can crowd out this consciousness, and do, but to maintain the consciousness of the Divine Presence in our daily life is the greatest possible of our achievements and ought therefore to be the chief business of our life. Otherwise we lower ourselves in the standard of our being and fall far short of achieving in life that which was within the range of our possibilities.

The potentiality which enables us to attain to this consciousness, we call faith. Mr. Corbin speaks of a faith "irrational and unanswerable." The terms cannot be applied to Christian faith, the faith founded on the teachings of Jesus.

The realm of faith is the supernatural, and bears the same relation to the spirit-life as seeing, hearing, and all the other senses bear to the nature-life. The student of science goes down to the realm of nature to make discoveries concerning what it is, what work it does, and how it does its work. To make these discoveries, sense and reason are his equipment. So the student of the supernatural. He, too, has certain questions to ask, and for which he desires answer. Are we a part of the supernatural? Is the supernatural a part of us?

What relationship does the supernatural bear to us? What relationship ought we to bear to the supernatural?

Sense and reason cannot invade the realm of the supernatural and bring us back the answers. Faith alone can, and does this. Why should we refuse to believe that our spirit-life cannot be endued with a power to tell us whether or not there is a supernatural? Whether or not we are a part of it? Whether or not it is a part of us?

While sense and reason, observation and human experience cannot create this faith, nor take the place of it, nevertheless these all are essential in order that faith may be confirmed to us as faith. Belief which is not confirmed by human experience is not faith. It is credulity; the credulity now in no small measure stalking on the top of this earth and arrogating to itself the name of faith. Faith never deceives us; never disappoints us. Credulity may, but faith never. The nature-life of man does not live apart from his spirit—life; nor his spirit-life apart from his nature-life, not in this earthly sphere at any rate. So faith, without the confirmations of sense and reason and the collective experiences of mankind, has no place nor value in the practical affairs of human life. The business of religion is therefore something more than to profess a faith. Its business is to bring confirmation in respect to that which is called faith, so that the certitude that this, which we call faith, is faith and not mere credulity.

Christ, as has been said, is our authority in respect to all things supernatural and he will continue so until a greater than he appears on the stage of action. First among other things, he took issue with the concept of God which was in vogue among his people at that time. The attribute of "wrath," which was the chief trait of character of God as viewed by the Jewish nation preceding his day, this he entirely eliminated from his concept. Following the lead set by this Master Mind, we are dropping this attribute out also as fast as we can get the people to believe the truth of the Christ-concept of God as a God of "Love."

Of this better and more rational concept, we find daily confirmations of the truth of it from the daily occurrences of our daily life. Our sense and reason both bear witness to the truth of it. The collective experiences of mankind, bear witness to the truth of it. So, also, confirms truth, not by the works which he did yesterday, but by those which He is doing to-day, and among these the progress which is being made towards a world-wide brotherhood is not the least.

Confirmation of our faith comes also through the realization of the other potentialities with which faith is associated. Among these, emanating from our spirit—life, the three greatest, we are told by one of the most aggressive and observant of the early followers of Jesus, are, faith and its two associates, hope and love.

Hope has especially to do with the to-morrow of our life it visualizes the future and brings to us a sense of security, an expectation that to-morrow will be as to-day, only better. Hope makes the journey of life ahead of us and sees our future filled with the good things which God has provided and has in store ready for our every need. The to-morrow of our life, as was Canaan to Joshua and his companions, is a land of plenty. We may, therefore, face that to-morrow with fearless hearts because of that which hope has to tell us concerning it. Powers and influences are at work to make provision for our needs, needs which have to be met, but which we, like new-born babes, cannot meet ourselves by anything which we now possess or can command. When the need arises, however, the requisite provision to meet it is there. How could this be unless there was an Over-seeing Mind making ready beforehand the provisions required to meet these needs? There is nothing haphazard in life. When we reach its tomorrow, it is as our hope declared it would be, the same as today, only better.

These confirmations of faith and hope are every-day occurrences in our life. They are not for one member of the race only, but for all. The rain falls upon the just and the unjust, the deserving and the undeserving. Nothing is left to chance. Everything is well-planned and well-disposed, both for the present and the future. The to-morrow of our life will be as to-day because the Provider goeth before us to prepare the way. It will be better than to-day because of the law irrevocable and unchangeable associated with life, and without which there is no life—THOU SHALT GROW—the law of advance and progress.

To live in reliance upon God and His laws will bring us to that state of mind in which fear will find no place in our life. Let it be remembered, however, that God discloses himself only through our potentialities. He brings to gift into our life except though the exercise of these. We are not parasites living on the goodness and mercy of God only, but are co-workers with Him. Follow the urge of your faith and the vision of your hope and be confirmed in your mind that as the promise, so is the performance on the part of God. Make a tryst with your partner every morning of your life, follow the lead which your faith and your hope give, and the day will not end disastrously nor tragically, but in the achievement of a God-appointed triumph. When your need remains a need, unremedied, un-met, still follow the urge and the vision. The future, not the past, is your great heritage. The to-morrow of your life is fraught with great promise, but the day after to-morrow is fraught with still greater. This is the message and the command which hope brings to all, not one excepted.

Once more, our faith is confirmed by another associate, the greatest of them all, the power to love power to feel that over us and around us, as well as within us, is God, the Supernatural One, bearing towards us a spirit of good will; carrying with Him a promise of guidance, protection and safety; possessing toward us the feeling which a true father bears towards his own children, and continuing to bear this feeling, no matter how unnatural or irresponsive his offspring may be to him—to realize that there is such a love in God, to be confident that this love will always be at our service, to have our hearts responding in an alike spirit to this concept of Him, to have our minds convinced of its truth, to have our souls snuggling under its protection in safety, this is the greatest achievement possible to man.

The next is like unto it, to love our fellowman as we love ourselves. Herein is a potentiality which is to be exercised not merely towards those from whom we expect to get a return for our services equal to that which we give, not merely to be a neighbour to those who will be neighbour to us, towards those who are our well-wishers and friends, but to all men without exception with whom we are brought in contact as associates in life. It requires of us a service to our enemies equal to that which we ought and are prepared to render our friends. No matter how far short others may be falling from this relationship, no matter though they may be persons from whose evil doings we are made the sufferers, our example in this is to be God, the Eternal Father, not man. If He, the Eternal Father, is expected to, and does, love, forgive, and show mercy to the unthankful, the immoral, the criminal, the degraded, and all the derelicts in all the stages of their dereliction, so must we in all our relationships to our fellowmen. Herein is something in which no man can be example unto us. The pattern after whom we are to plan and follow out our life in respect to this potentiality is that of the Father Himself. His is the ideal spirit. In respect to this potentiality, there cannot be a half-measure of attainment. The goal set for us, is the goal which God has set for Himself. "Be ye perfect, even as your Father in heaven is perfect," This is the goal set for man, according to the challenge and testimony of Christ.

Finally, these three associate potentialities, have a fourth which must be exemplified in every-day life if these three are to achieve their realization. This is the power to know good from evil. There is a right and a wrong course of life, and to us is given the power to know the right from the wrong. To us is given the assurance that good will follow from doing that which is right, but that evil comes into our life from following that which is wrong. If a man will not be taught this by the hearing of the ear, by placing confidence in, and following the teaching of those who know, then he will be taught it by experience, and a dearly-bought knowledge this oftentimes is. But whether discovered in the one way or the other, discovered it will be to every man who walketh upon the face of this earth. The lesson that evil is evil, and though destined to be, and yet one day it will be, eliminated from the life of man, yet it will not be eliminated, nor will it allow itself to be eliminated until it has done all the evil it can to the man who was unwise enough to choose the evil instead of the good, the wrong course of life instead of the right. TO LEARN TO DO WELL: TO CEASE TO DO EVIL—this is man's great vocation in life.

There is but one God, the God from whom both man and the great Teacher of Nazareth derived their potentiality, the potentiality which determines our mission in life; the God who created the universe and the earth as a part of the universe; the God who created man upon the earth and each man a part of that creation; the God who created powers by means of which continuance and perfection is being given to His plans and purposes in respect to everything upon this earth, promising protection to all, not one excepted; this God, in accord with the concept of Him revealed by Christ, is a GOD OF LOVE.

There is a supernatural world, but it is not greater than the God who created it. Of this world we may not know everything, but we can know enough to enable us to learn life's great lesson, "TO LEARN TO DO WELL: TO CEASE TO DO EVIL"; and this, not because there is, or there is not, a pit of torture for the wicked wicked, but because good is good and evil is evil. We choose to do good because it is good. We refrain from evil because it is evil.

The ways of God are not hidden from man, Nature declares His handiworks and manifests His laws, one of which at least is not hidden and to which the experience of all men bears ample testimony, "Whatsoever a man soweth, that shall he also reap."

It is good for us to discover what were the ideas and ideals which Christ released and taught mankind for their guidance. This knowledge is good, and next to knowing, there is nothing better than following them. But not all those who profess to be personifying the teacher are so doing. Not all those who are professing to represent their exemplar, are truthfully doing so. His teachings, as has been said, have suffered additions, emendations and barnacle encrustments, and to believe these and to follow them is not good. It is evil and the worst form of all evil. The people in this country and the country south of us are turning away from the teachings of the professed representatives of this great teacher, and their numbers have now reached the tragical proportions of incredible millions. Is it because of these emendations, additions and barnacle encrustments? Is it because the children of truth have come asking for bread and are being offered a stone as a substitute? Is it because, when asking for fish, they are being dealt out scorpions?

This is the question that is now being asked by those who have the interests of the kingdom of God at heart, as they see these millions deserting their Churches in the United States and in Canada. They have gone out and they will not return until they receive the truth and nothing but the truth; until they see in these Churches exemplification of the brotherhood which Christ instituted and which he declared was to become world-wide in its scope. The musician cannot play until he gets back his instrument. The student cannot go on in his quest for knowledge until he gets back his books. The pilgrim will not be able to find his way across the desert plain until he has secured the services of a guide.

The great question, the greatest of all questions, will not eliminate itself. It will continue the greatest until it receives adequate answer, adequate at least for this life's needs— WHAT IS TRUTH?

Down the ages there cometh to us the answer, but in the form of a command:

"THOU SHALT LOVE THE LORD THY GOD WITH ALL THY HEART, AND WITH ALL THY SOUL, AND WITH ALL THY MIND. AND, THOU SHALT LOVE THY NEIGHBOUR AS THYSELF."

A life of faith and hope and love,
A life which comes from God,
The life which cannot fade in death,
We live it now with God.

We'll live a life of love;
We'll live a life of love;
We'll live a life of love;
The life enjoined by God.

The life which triumphs over wrong,
The life from sin set free,
The life the greatest man can live,
We live it now with Thee.

So give us grace to work and pray,
A trust to make us strong;
A power of hope to open eye,
And love that ends all wrong.

Moffatt's translation of the New Testament.

THE LAST POST

IT WAS TWO HOURS past midnight when a message came requesting me to go to a home several miles distant, where lay a young man dying, on this occasion also, from that same dread malady, tuberculosis.

The month was March, and the north-west wind blew coldly against my face as I drove along the mud road to the home. The moistened soil, congealing on the wheels of the buggy, made driving hard for the horse, who tugged steadily and uncomplainingly at the task set for him at so unusual an hour. But these things mattered nought. The hour was fraught with momentous issue to a unit of the human family, every one of whom, we are taught to believe, is a precious gem in the universal scheme of God. When I arrived at the home, I opened the door gently—I was an oft visitor at that home— and beheld in a small room opposite, a dim lamp burning, revealing to me, sitting by the bedside and keeping her last and lonely vigil, the mother of this, her only child.

The young man was the first to observe my entrance. Turning his head, he smiled expectantly. As soon as I was entered, he discovered to me the reason why he had asked me to come at that unusual hour. It was not that I might be the messenger of comfort to that home, but that the young man might be given the opportunity to make request that, through me, he might deliver his last message to his family, to his friends friends and to his neighbours, the little world in which he lived and moved and had his being, during the short years he was permitted to live upon this earth.

Pointing to a Bible on a near-by shelf, he asked his mother to hand it to him. Opening it at a place marked, he put his white and wasted finger beside a certain verse and said,

"I want you to preach my funeral sermon from this text."

Looking down, this is what I read: "I am persuaded that neither death, nor life, nor angels, nor principalities, nor powers, nor things present, nor things to come, nor height, nor depth, nor any other creature, shall be able to separate us from the love of God, which is in Christ Jesus, Our Lord."

Can we believe that there is such a love, and at the same time believe that there are created human beings, God's own natural offspring, destined to hope their career outside the pale of this faith, this hope, and this love?

Only if the Great Drama of Human Life is to end, not in triumph, but in failure and tragedy.

Only if the God, in whom we trust, is not our Father, perfect in His love, bestowing forgiveness and mercy upon all who need that forgiveness and mercy.

Only if recover of man is not possible with God.

Only if the Eternal Love can be perfect and not make all mankind the Eternal Beneficiaries of His Eternal Love.

The Hope that sees in the To-morrow of human life failure and tragedy is not the Hope of the present-day, enlightened Christianity.

ABOUT THE AUTHOR

Rev. Hugh Cowan (May 20, 1867 – April 19, 1943) was a Presbyterian Church of Canada and later United Church of Canada minister, author, editor and historian.

Hugh Cowan was born on May 20, 1867 in Bentinck, Ontario, Canada to John Cowan and Mary McLean both of whom were born in Scotland.

John and Mary McLean Cowan

In 1893, he finished his Bachelor of Arts degree in Manitoba College. He pursued his Master of Arts at Knox College, Toronto in 1896. He later pursued his Bachelor of Divinity degree at Kingston, Ontario's Queen's Theological College and graduated in 1905.

During Cowan's first ministry at Rutherford Presbyterian Church in Dawn-Euphemia near Chatham, Ontario, he met Jean Eloise Wood who lived at nearby Langbank. They were married on October 31, 1899 in London, Ontario.

Hugh Cowan and Jean Eloise Wood had three daughters and six sons. James Alexander Cowan, Marjorie Jean Cowan Jolliffe, John Kenneth Cowan, Hugh Raymond Cowan, Mary Elizabeth Cowan, Grace Edith Cowan Fitzpatrick, Stuart McLean Cowan, Donald Murray Cowan and Alan Wood Cowan

Hugh and Jean Cowan

Church ministry

Cowan was ordained by the Chatham Presbytery of the Presbyterian Church of Canada in August 17, 1897.

Cowan served as a pastor in Oakdale United Church (formerly known as Oakdale Presbyterian Church), and Rutherford Presbyterian Church in Lambton County from 1897 to 1900, in St. Andrew's Presbyterian Church in North Easthope and Shakespeare Presbyterian Church in Shakespeare, Perth County, Ontario from 1900 to 1905, a minister in charge of St. Paul's Presbyterian Church in Harwich Township, Kent County, Ontario, Bethel Presbyterian Church, and The Ridge Presbyterian Church from 1905 to 1913, in Haynes Ave. Church in St. Catharines from 1914 to 1916, Chalmer's Presbyterian Church in Toronto from 1919 to 1921, and in High Park Presbyterian Church in 1922.

From 1925 to 1937, in various congregations of the United Church of Canada, he served as a minister at Bethel United Church near Chatham, Ontario, as a pastor at MacLennan, Desbarats and Port Rock near Sault Ste. Marie, and Sault Suburban Church area charge in Sault Ste. Marie.

Cowan has authored numerous historical books. One was *Canadian Achievement in the Province of Ontario – The Detroit River District* where he wrote about the history of the Canadian people in Detroit River area including Essex county and Windsor, Ontario. The book was recently republished as Ontario and the Detroit Frontier 1701-1814. A similar unpublished work on the history of Chatham and Kent County was also written.

He created *Gold and Silver Jubilee, Sault Ste. Marie, Canada* detailing more the history of Sault Ste. Marie. A monthly publication Mer Douce was produced for three years and is one of the important historical references for the Manitoulin Island, Georgian Bay and Muskoka areas.

He also wrote a fictional book entitled *La Cloche. The Story of Hector MacLeod and His Misadventures in the Georgian Bay and the La Cloche Districts* which is an adventure tale.

Jean and Hugh Cowan

Cowan also published this book centering on the progress of Christianity called *The Great Drama of Human Life.*

Cowan served as the managing editor of Algonquin Historical Society of Canada.

He retired in 1937.

Hugh Cowan's Wikipedia article is at http://en.wikipedia.org/wiki/Hugh_Cowan

Hugh Cowan died at the General and Marine Hospital in Owen Sound, Ontario on April 19, 1943 at the age of 73.

Silverwoods
Publishing

Made in the USA
Las Vegas, NV
02 July 2022

51024799R00075